Dear Freda & Peter,

"Serve the Lord fervently,"
Rom. 12:11

Blessings,

Dennis Ngien

A Faith Worth
Believing, Living, and Commending

A Faith Worth
Believing, Living, and Commending

DENNIS NGIEN

WIPF & STOCK · Eugene, Oregon

A FAITH WORTH BELIEVING, LIVING, AND COMMENDING

www.wipfandstock.com

ISBN 13: 978-1-55635-681-0

Manufactured in the U.S.A.

For mentors, pastors, students, and friends
of Centre for Mentorship and Theological Reflection
on its tenth anniversary,
with gratitude for your partnership in the gospel.

Contents

Foreword

A SPECIALIST HAS BEEN defined as one who gets to know more and more about less and less, and there are people in academia whom the cap seems to fit. An ethos of competitive specialization affects leading centers of learning, and in a world like ours, where employment and promotion patterns mesh with original sin to produce and maintain rivalry, this state of affairs is likely to continue. As leaders in their own field, however, specialists are valuable persons.

A generalist has a different profile. The description that fits him is that he gets to know more and more about—not less and less, but more and more, though usually not at specialist level. Human life around him is ordinarily the focus of his interest; breadth rather than detail is ordinarily the mark of his speaking and writing. Academically his goal is less to push out the walls of knowledge than to relate and synthesize different aspects of life, for ordinarily he is a people-person rather than an abstract thinker. Pastors, counselors, and schoolmasters are usually generalists; their nurturing role requires them so to be. They gather and apply wisdom, and in doing this they too become more marketable and perhaps valuable.

Dennis Ngien of Tyndale University College and Seminary is a generalist. Pastor, evangelist, apologist, teacher, researcher, and founder of the Centre for Mentorship and Theological Reflection, he is a versatile, ten-talented man of God. One of his main academic resources is Luther, much of whose own evangelical strength and wisdom has rubbed off on him. The occasional, fugitive pieces that the present book gathers give a fair indication of his range and quality, and they will be read, I predict, with equal pleasure and benefit to the thoughtful reader. I heartily commend this collection.

J. I. Packer
Board of Governors' Professor of Theology, Regent College, Vancouver
Senior Scholar, Centre for Mentorship and Theological Reflection
Toronto

Acknowledgments

SPECIAL THANKS MUST BE extended to several scholars and intimates: Dr. J. I. Packer, renowned theologian, for his generous foreword; Dr. Jeffrey Greenman, Associate Dean of Wheaton College, Dr. Janet Clark, Academic Dean of Tyndale Seminary, Dr. Kevin Livingston, Senior Pastor of Knox Presbyterian Church in Toronto, and Dr. Ken Gamble (MD), Executive Director of Missionary Health Institute, for their keen commendations; Dr. Matthew Knell, for his editorial work; and Ada Chung for her labor in formatting at the initial stage. All of them have invested many hours of reading and offered helpful suggestions, which ensure that the text is clear and readable. Any weaknesses in the book I shall not impute to them, but to myself, who is learning how to write in a way that ignites in readers a hunger for God, his word, his people, and the lost world.

Chapter 2, "The God Who Suffers" (February 1997), and chapter 7, "Picture Christ: Martin Luther's Advice on Preparing to Die" (April 2007), were published in *Christianity Today*. Chapter 5, "Learning Preaching from a Hero of Faith," is a shorter version of a larger article, "Theology of Preaching in Martin Luther," which was published in *Themelios* 28 (2003). I am grateful to these journals for allowing me to reuse these works here.

This book was compiled during a distressing time when my father-in-law was battling the advanced stages of cancer. My beloved wife, Ceceilia and her mother were dedicated wholeheartedly to the care of their devoted father and husband, who is now in God's abode. Yet they still had the stamina and spirit to be with our son, Hansel, so that I could focus on writing. Credit must be given to them, without whom this book would not have been completed. I thank God for Hansel, especially his cheerful disposition and hilarious humor by which I am rescued from innumerable lapses into discouragement and distraction at this time of trials and anxieties. His wish that he might be the first to hold this book, which has now been fulfilled, served as a powerful impetus towards completing it.

A Faith Worth Believing, Living, and Commending

To God Be the Glory!

Dennis Ngien
September 6, 2007

Introduction

MANY PEOPLE HAVE TRIED persuading me to publish my sermons or talks, especially those that are frequently cited, quoted, or requested. In commemoration of the tenth anniversary of the Centre for Mentorship and Theological Reflection (see appendix) in 2008, as its founder, I have compiled a few representative pieces in a chronological order. This collection is the fruit of many years of preaching, teaching, and mentoring. The materials presented here are reflections on a variety of topics: a belief in God's suffering and the pastoral implications of this, Luther's theology of preaching, practical approaches to evangelistic preaching, pastoral advice on death and dying, apologetic preaching as done by Paul in a post-Christian culture, effective living in the power of the Holy Spirit, striking a balance between enthusiastic service and fervent love, the image of God's love in the Old Testament, and personal exhortations. With variations, they were delivered on different occasions such as an evangelistic crusade, a spiritual convention, an ecumenical conference (the Centre's annual event), and graduation chapel; and to diverse audiences including: scholars, professors, seminary students, young people, and the Centre delegates. Although aimed primarily at non-specialists, the materials presented here interweave theological substance, biblical interpretation, and practical implications.

Reflective of the Centre's distinctive is the interface of theology and piety. In this, there is no apparent contradiction between being a doctor (PhD) and a preacher, a scholar and a mentor, a professor and a pastor, for they are all inseparably one. In churches dominated by the spirit of anti-intellectualism and subjective experience, this book is a correction to such extremes. Dr. John Mackay, the former president of Princeton Theological Seminary, once remarked aptly: "Commitment without reflection is fanaticism in action. But reflection without commitment is the paralysis of all action."[1] This collection is proof of a causal connection

1. Quoted in John Stott, *Your Mind Matters*, 60. Downers Grove, IL: InterVarsity,

between theological reflection and passionate commitment. Although it was written on the balcony of my own study where reflection and meditation are carried out, it is cognizant of ministry contexts where people's needs and struggles are most evident. Every facet of life, Henry Blackaby, my first mentor, said, is indicative of God's triumphant grace, and thus an occasion for experiencing God. With anecdotes and analyses, the readers will be enabled to discern the signs of divine transcendence in their lives, and to apprehend, or rather to be apprehended by, the beauty of God's grace, the abiding basis of our being and well-being.

Seeking to be a true theologian, I give heed to the words of Charles Simeon, "For the attainment of divine knowledge we are directed to combine a dependence on God's Spirit with our own researches. Let us, then, not presume to separate what God has thus united."[2] A true theologian must allow the priority of biblical revelation to set the agenda, and be the basis of sound theological formulations. Likewise, a true preacher should not allow human reason to rise above the real teacher, the Holy Spirit, and become his own teacher. Such is the practice of some preachers who delude themselves into thinking that the Scriptures are subject to them and can be easily grasped by their mind, as if they were a human production like other writings for which no Spirit or prayers were needed.

What has been written in this book reveals the heartbeat of a mentor, who earnestly hungers for divine beauty and holiness, whose hunger God eagerly fulfills, just as he promises, and who wishes the same for his readers. The basic assumption in this book is *a faith that is worth believing is a faith that is worth living, and thus worth commending*. The book is also an exercise of faith seeking understanding, whose understanding only God can supply. It is written with the hope that it will lead readers from knowing God to loving him, then enjoying him, and finally proclaiming him so that others will be brought into the orbit of God's inestimable grace. Not until our hearts, which God's heart touches, touch the heart of others is our ministry complete, and our life found pleasing to him.

1972.
  2. Ibid., 7.

1

Paul's Apologetic Preaching at Mars Hill
(Acts 17:16–34) *

S T. PAUL WAS ON the move again—often the victim of persecution, re-
vilement, and cruelty—despite his good experience with the nobles
of Berea. He was forced to leave because those that treated him harshly,
while he ministered in Thessalonica, had perused him. He fled to Athens,
leaving behind Silas and Timothy to tend to the young church. The evangelistic team was broken up. Paul was forlorn in the alien culture of a
colossal city engrossed with idolatry.

As he was walking around the streets of Athens, he was profoundly
anxious. Torn apart within because every corner he turned he saw idols.
He was greatly concerned that God should be honored, firmly convinced
that Jesus Christ is Lord and Savior. But as he looked around the city, he
saw no understanding of God as God, no evidence of the glory going
to God, and no conviction that Jesus is the Savior. His heart was deeply
stirred because wherever he went he saw more gods than anything else.

Heart Roused into Action

Henry Martin, the missionary to India, had a dream in which he saw Jesus
prostrating at the foot of a Hindu deity. He said, "That excited in me more
horror than I could ever express. I was cut to the soul at that blasphemy. I
could not endure existence if Jesus were not glorified. It would be hell for
me if Jesus would be so dishonored."

Now we could be emotionally disturbed and not be moved to do
anything. When Paul was emotionally distressed, what did he do? Acts

* With some variations, this sermon was frequently delivered in former Soviet Union,
former Eastern Europe, Africa, and Asia, and over a decade of evangelistic ministry
(1991–2000).

17:17 says, "Therefore he reasoned with the Jews and the devout Greeks in the synagogue and daily in the marketplace." Idols aroused in Paul an inner compulsion to debate, witness, and preach. His usual practice was to go to the Jewish synagogue on Saturday; where he tried to convince the Jews that Jesus Christ was the Messiah, as promised in the Old Testament. Then between Sunday and the following Saturday, he did not stand idle. Instead he would go to the marketplace, in the open air, and reason daily with any people who might be there.

Word spread and many people gathered around Paul to hear him. Verse 21 says, "The Athenians and foreigners stayed around doing nothing, but telling and hearing something new." Paul's preaching drew the highly educated and articulate Athenian philosophers down to the marketplace to hear him.

Epicurean and Stoic Philosophies

Epicurean and Stoic philosophy were prevalent in Greece, at the time. The Epicureans were the materialists, according to whom pleasure was the chief goal of life. But the only pleasure worth possessing was a life of tranquility, free from pain and anxiety. The Epicureans pursued a simple life with reasoned and moderated indulgence. Their sole preoccupation is with this earthly life, for there is no after-life from which to fear or hope. God, if he exists, dwells in eternal calm, utterly transcendent and completely uninvolved in the lives of people.

On the contrary, the Stoics were the pantheists, according to whom reality is one, without distinction, that God is all, and all is God. Adherents to the new-age movement are pantheists. Shirley Maclean claimed to have discovered the truth about herself, and concluded, "I am God." For the Stoics, the only good is to follow one's reason and be self-sufficient, unmoved by inner feeling or outward circumstances. All other things—life, death, pleasure, and pain—were indifferent, neither good nor evil. The Stoics espoused ethics characterized by self-control, obedience, and duty. Although they affirmed with Paul the immanence of God, they repudiated his assertion that history has an end, moving from the time of ignorance to that of repentance, and finally to the day of judgment.

These two groups of philosophers were present in the marketplace. As Paul began to speak, they gave him a hard time. Some asked, "What on earth is this babbler trying to say?" Others said, "He seems to be preaching

rather strange gods, because Paul was preaching about Jesus and the resurrection" (v. 18). So they gave Paul a very special invitation: "Come to the
Areopagus" (v.19); "we want to hear the new teachings you are preaching
for they are strange ideas to our ears" (v.20).

The Areopagus is a hill that overlooks the marketplace. The Latin
translation is Mars Hill, and it was the place where people went to phi-
losophize and was once the meeting place of the Athenian court. Paul was
invited to appear there, no doubt for public session but not necessarily in
the form of a legal trial. The occasion gave him the opportunity to explain
the true God.

Building Bridges

Despite all the perversity Paul saw in their idols he began his address
with a positive and complimentary note about Athenian spirituality.
Verse 22 reads, "You men of Athens, I perceive that in every way you are
very religious." This may seem ironic but Paul sought to build bridges
and did not try to take God's role as judge. He did not say, "You men of
Athens, I perceive that in every way, you are wrong, and you are going
to hell" or "in every way, I know the truth, and you don't, and if you
keep quiet, I will tell you the truth." Instead, he commended them for
their religiosity. To earn the right to be heard, a double portion of tact
is required. There should not be any offense in us. The offense is in the
gospel. Christ himself is the stumbling block, not us.

Unbelievers cannot absorb the content of the Bible if its message
is obscured by objectionable attitudes and behavior. An Indian proverb
illustrates this, "When you cut off a person's nose, there is no use to give
him a rose to smell." A skilled English hunter was having trouble killing
birds and said to his attendant, "Today is just not my day . . . I did not
shoot well, did I?" Smilingly, the attendant replied, "I beg to disagree. It
isn't that you are shooting poorly, but that God is merciful towards the
birds." The attendant's reply showed the kind of tact Paul used even as
he was agitated by Athens's excessive idolatry. His positive introduction
provided an appropriate entry point for his address.

Paul's discovery of the most honest altar with the inscription "To
the unknown god" (v. 23) shattered him. It is terribly sad for someone to
build an altar and not even know the object of their worship. Though part
of Paul may have been grieved he capitalized on the Athenian's apparent

deep desire, commitment and this particular ray of honesty he saw in their worship. The craftsman had no idea which way to begin, except to set up an altar with the inscription: "To the unknown god." Paul perceived the positives and negatives and eagerly seized the inscription as a way to introduce the reality behind this "unknown god" of the Athenians. He provided an answer that met with their deepest desire of God, about whom they did not know anything. How utterly lost in their philosophies these people were! To a person who worships God ignorantly, Paul said in verse 23, "Whom therefore you ignorantly worship, him declare I unto you." He declared to them the true God so that their religion would not be devoid of meaning and content, and their devotion may have direction and basis.

Paul is a great master at making use of these pagan ideas as a bridge or a starting point of contact for gospel proclamation. He understood the ways and cultural milieu of the Athenian people. He was well-versed in Greek philosophy, and perceived glimmers of truth in their pagan philosophy. Later in the text, he quoted their ideas, turning them into another point of contact for gospel preaching. Furthermore, he quoted pagan ideas to expose their errors, and destroy their own system of idolatry (vv. 28–29).

Athenian Ignorance Exposed

For Paul, God cannot be rightly worshipped except as he is known. The Athenian problem, which Paul identified, was their ignorant worship. With audacity and skill, he set them right about their conceptions of God with a view which would lead them toward efficacious worship. There are three things concerning God of which they were totally ignorant.

The first thing they were ignorant of is the fact that God cannot be domesticated and confined to a certain locality. The Athenians believed in a god with a regional domain. Their city contained beautiful architecture that made it easy to discern where deity dwelled. The second misconception is that we must appease God with gifts. This notion implies that power for salvation is in our hands. Finally, the Athenians believed that God needs us.

God neither dwells in buildings made by men, nor is he to be worshipped with things men offer him; nor does he need anything from men. God is not helpless; we are, and we need him. Their view of god is with handicaps, like a disabled mother who is put in a beautiful nursing home—because she cannot visit people, people have to come and visit her during visiting hours. Paul's dialogue shows them their erroneous beliefs and an all powerful, self sufficient, omnipresent being that we are lost without. He said,

> So Paul, standing in the midst of the Areopagus, said: 'Men of Athens, I perceive that in every way you are very religious. For as I passed along and observed the objects of your worship, I found also an altar with this inscription, 'To the unknown god.' What therefore you worship as unknown, this I proclaim to you. The God who made the world and everything in it, being Lord of heaven and earth, does not live in temples made by man, nor is he served by human hands, as though he needed anything, since he himself gives to all mankind life and breath and everything. And he made from one man every nation of mankind to live on all the face of the earth, having determined allotted periods and the boundaries of their dwelling place, that they should seek God, in the hope that they might feel their way toward him and find him. Yet he is actually not far from each one of us, for, "In him we live and move and have our being'; as even some of your own poets have said, 'For we are indeed his offspring." (Acts 17:22–28, ESV)

The only way we can worship correctly is by taking freely that which he offers us. If we think we can give God anything of value without first receiving from him all that we need, we are like the Athenians, who worshipped God ignorantly. We can give him only what he has first given. This is borne out in Psalm 116:12–13: "What shall I give to the Lord for all that he has given unto me? I'll take the cup of salvation." True worship consists in offering God the sacrifice of thanksgiving that is rightly due him.

True Knowledge of God Expounded

After outlining the errors of the Athenian system, Paul positively pointed out things they really needed to know about God in order that they might worship God correctly. This, said Calvin, explained why Paul in his Areopagus sermon in verse 24 "makes a beginning with a definition of God, so that he might prove from that how God ought to be worshipped, because the one thing depends upon the other."[1] The knowledge of God, which is the presupposition of true worship, is spelled out in verses 24–29.

---

1. See Calvin's Commentary on Acts 17:25 as cited in John Witvliet, *Worship Seeking Understanding*, 152. Grand Rapids: Baker Academic, 2003.

First, God is the creator (v. 24). God created the universe and all that is in it. He did it alone, without the use of any pre-existent materials. He did it *ex nihilo*, i.e., without the use of any antecedent causes, without human advice or assistance. He did not have any engine but his own word; he did not have any pattern but his own mind. The world and all that is in it are the effects of divine causality. God commanded this universe into being by his own speech, which is his own action.

Secondly, God is the Lord of heaven and earth (v. 24). He is just as active in ruling and sustaining this universe as in creating it. The same power that created the vast universe holds all things together in the palm of his hand. This God does not grow weary, nor does he have the capacity to dissipate. This is set in stark contrast with the Athenian conception of God, in which God is worshipped in temples made by men. Today you can still go to the magnificent Parthenon, one of the masterpieces of human ingenuity. The Parthenon was meant to be God's dwelling place, a place of free worship where people could come and worship whatever they wanted. In truth though it was a temple built to glorify human achievement rather than God.

Magnificent as the Parthenon is, God does not live there. Neither does he fit into any human pattern; nor can he be represented by creaturely or created things. As the uncreated God, he made and sustains heaven and earth and all things therein. He is utterly immense, and completely infinite. There is no place in his creation in which he is not, or from which he is excluded. He fills the universe with his presence, yet remains distinct from it. This runs contrary to the Stoic Pantheistic conception of God, in which Creator and creation merge into one, as a drop of water dissolves into the vast ocean.

One of the implications of asserting that God is the Creator and Lord is that a distinction must be drawn between God and his creations. To illustrate, the painter and painting are distinct, not to be confused. To worship aright is to worship the God of creation, unlike the Athenians who worship his creations, and thus worship wrongly. There is a natural tendency, because of sin, to serve "the created things rather than the Creator" (cf. Rom 1:25), thereby merging the creator and the creation.

Next, God is the giver and we are the recipients of all his gifts. We are in the presence of the God who gives us "life, breath and everything else" (v. 25). God is the source of our being and the sustainer of our well-being. Everything we have comes from him; we do not give to him as if he needs

6

anything from us. We do not help him out. There is no lack or deficiency or contingency in God's being. He does not depend on us for something he does not possess, for he is infinitely resourceful. We do not enrich or enhance God's being by what we give him. He is the divine sovereign, the creator and ruler of this universe, the giver, who is self-sufficient, independent of us, and needs nothing from us. With these assertions, Paul discredits the rampant idolatry of the Athenians. God as God does not need us to do any spiritual routines, as if his being requires them. We are absolutely contingent upon God, the giver of life, breath and everything. It is to God alone that we owe our very being and well-being: "For from him, and through him, and to him are all things. To him be the Glory!" (Rom 11:36)

Fourth, God is the governor and controller of nations and history. Verse 26 reads: "From one man or one source God makes every nation of men to settle on the face of the earth." That alone would have been a shock to the Athenians, according to whom the world consists of only two kinds: the Greeks and the barbarians. They were the super-race, the international hotshots. But Paul declared that we are of the same family tree, whatever race or color we are. God even "determined the times set for them and the exact places where they should live" (v. 26b). He is controlling history and the destiny of men and nations. He planned the exact times when nations should rise and fall. He also planned the specific area to be occupied by each nation.

John Wesley has a good biblical outlook. He said, "I read the newspapers to see how God is governing his world." History is on schedule, because God is running it. This perspective is a refutation of the Epicureans who thought that everything happens by chance; it is also a repudiation of the Stoics who thought things happen by fate; and it is also a rejection of modern secular science which does not acknowledge a higher power or authority over them and all their investigations.

Fifth, God, though transcendent, is immanently near to each one of us. There is a purpose clause in verse 27: "God did this *so that* men would seek him, and feel after him and find him." Everything God has done—the creating and sustaining of the universe, the giving of life, breath and everything, and all that he is doing in history and for nations—is geared towards one end, that men may seek him in the hope of finding him. This is the climax of Paul's sermon. God's objective in creation, in preservation, in providence, and in history is to reveal himself so that men may see that revelation and follow after him and find him.

The nearness of God is the main point Paul intended to communicate. In other words, the Athenians do not have to be trapped in their ignorant worship, for God can be intelligently known, and thus rightly worshipped. Our indwelling father, God, has supplied the very contents of who he is so that they could worship him by the knowledge he has given them. This is the liberating news which Paul wanted the Athenians to embrace as a way out of their impotent worship.

In parts of the world where the gospel is not heard, do people still possess the revelation of God? Of course, as his offspring God is not far from each one of us, and can be found. He reveals himself to all creatures. No one who desires it is deprived of the knowledge of God. Jeremiah 29:13 affirms, "You shall seek me and find me when you search me with all your hearts." Psalm 145:18–19 also puts it affirmatively: "The Lord is near to those who call upon him, and to all who call upon him in truth. He'll fulfill the desires of those who fear him; he will hear their cries and save them."

What will happen to the pagans? If they really seek to know God, God will hear their cries and save them. God does not hold people responsible for what they do not know. God has put himself on display in the world so that men may search after him and find him. To illustrate this, Paul pulled out two quotations from pagan Greek poetry in verse 28: "For in him we live and move and have our being." As some of your poets have said, "we are God's offspring." The first quotation ("For in him we live and move and have our being") came from Epimenides, and the second ("we are his offspring") from Aratus. The first quotation is an application to a pagan divinity named Zeus. Why did Paul quote this statement from Greek poetry that was originally applied to a pagan god? What Paul intended to say to the Greeks is this: look, your own poets, in their ignorance of the true God, afforded us infallible proof that God is knowable as the creator, sustainer, and the God of providence. Did not Epimenides say, by whatever name God is, that "it is in him we live, move and have our being?" Your own poet illustrates that God has revealed himself so that, even though they attach it to the wrong God, it is obvious to them that there is a God who makes them, holds all things together, and who takes care of them, even though they are ignorant of the God they desire to know.

And we came from him, as your own poet, Aratus, said, "We are God's offspring." Paul was emphatic that natural revelation is so obvious that the poets can see it, though they attach it to the wrong conception of

God. The revelation of God is so inherent in all of us, and so obvious to the pagans, even though it leads them to the wrong god.

Being well-versed in Greek philosophy, he quoted their ideas, utilizing them for the service of the gospel. He made use of the pagan ideas not only to expose their errors, but also to redirect their ignorant worship. This is evident in verse 29: "Therefore, since we are God's offspring, we should not think that the divine being is like gold or silver or stone—an image made by man." For God is not capable of any material representation; nor can he be reduced to the level of a creature. Paul thus called them to do away with their ignorant worship, and turn from their egocentricity or idolatry to the worship of the living God. Verse 30 reads: "In the past, God overlooked such ignorance, but now he commands all people everywhere to repent."

Finally, God is the judge. He has appointed a day and a person who will judge the world in righteousness. That person is Jesus Christ, the distinct Son of God, the Righteous One, "For he has set a day when he will judge the world with justice by the man he has appointed. He has given proof of this to all men by raising him from the dead" (v. 31). God has given them the assurance of his judgment. He even told them by whom he will judge, by the totally righteous one, Jesus Christ. You can be sure of this because God has raised him from the dead. Jesus Christ, the unique, distinct Son of God, the total righteousness, is the one who will judge. Therefore, we better repent. Paul said that the way they had gone about was a way of ignorance, which God had overlooked. Now repent, turn to the risen Christ, by whom the world will be judged.

Repentance is the missing note of so much preaching today. Paul preached it in Thessalonica, and here at Mars Hill. Why? Because God commands it. He did not allow his tact and understanding of pagan culture to interfere with the clear presentation of the gospel. He preached Jesus and his resurrection, the theme on which everything hinges. He was willing to love the Athenians. But when it came to the real issue, he did not compromise. He preached what God had commanded, even repentance, a theme which did not appeal to self-sufficient arrogant souls like the Stoics. They were prepared to hear philosophical arguments about God, to discuss or dispute with Paul. But something terminated the meeting, and it was the subject of Jesus and resurrection of the dead (v. 32).

Thoughts on Apologetic Preaching

There are three responses to Paul's sermon on the subject of the resurrection: (a) some sneered at it; (b) others said we will hear it again; and (c) a few believed, among them were Dionysius, a learned member of the Athenian court, who tradition said became the first Bishop of Athens, and also a woman named Damaris and a number of others. In light of these responses, I will conclude with a few practical pointers, which constitute a final word about apologetic preaching:

First, some argue that this is Paul's biggest failure, and his apologetics were a complete waste of time and effort. These people contend that his method was faulty and he blew it. I beg to differ, for Paul had no reason to believe that his labor was in vain. An intelligent apologist would know that, when dealing with the intellectuals, genuine results will always be few and far between. In my personal dialogue with intellectual Muslims and other religious adherents, the conversion rate has always been low.

Subsequently we must keep in mind that our responsibility as evangelists is not to persuade those who do not want to believe, but to make sure that everybody is given a chance to either *believe* or *disbelieve intelligently.* Those who believe will believe intelligently, and the rest who do not believe now have an opportunity to disbelieve intelligently, which they never had before. Thus we are to hold out the gospel so that the hearers are without excuse, and could not take refuge in the pretext of ignorance.

Next, as a working definition, apologetics is commending the truth of the gospel in such an attractive, scintillating, and relevant way that people are made to feel and think that Christianity may be true, not that it is true. Conversion is the work of the Holy Spirit while we just try to deliver the message. A practical question that often plagues the apologist is this, "how can I know that I have done the task of apologetic preaching?" If I can present the gospel to the post-Christian culture in such a way that makes my audience sit up and say, like the Athenians did, "I will hear you again, perhaps there are truths in Christianity I may have missed or misunderstood. I hope to search more," then I have done my job as an apologist. If we can create in others a thirst for the gospel, then rest assured that we have done a fairly good job as an apologist. Leave the result ultimately to the Holy Spirit, the power of the efficacy in the hearts of the hearers.

Finally, inasmuch as I admire the faithful apologists, and as often as I do apologetics, always bear in mind that we are not defending God, who needs no defense, but defending a belief system or our faith, as Paul did in Mars Hill. Apologetics, when it is defending God, is arrogant and idolatrous. Jesus is the great lion of Judah. You do not defend a lion; you just let it loose.

2

The God Who Suffers:
An Argument for God's Emotions[*]

IF GOD DOES NOT grieve, then can he love at all? Let me offer an argument for God's emotions.

DOES GOD EVER FEEL DISTRESSED?

The early Christian theologians said no. They accepted the Greek idea of divine impassibility, the notion that God cannot suffer since God stands outside the realm of human pain and sorrow. Philo, the Hellenistic Jewish theologian, had already assumed this in his understanding of Israel's God. Virtually all the early church fathers took it for granted, denying God any emotions because they might interrupt his tranquility. The Council of Chalcedon (AD 451) declared as "vain babblings" the idea that the divine nature could suffer, and it condemned those who believed it.

Like most theologians of Chalcedonian and earlier times, Calvin— and Reformed theology after him—assumed divine impassibility. The Westminster Confession of Faith explicitly asserted that God is "without body, parts, or passions, immutable." Similarly, a contemporary evangelical theologian argues that when Jesus died on the cross it was his human nature that suffered, not the divine.

But I would like to argue that this Greek notion that emotions or pain are unfit for deity is quite alien to biblical thought, and it leads to some unhappy results, as we will see.

---

* This article first appeared in *Christianity Today* (February, 1997). It was one of the thirteen timelessly significant articles posted in *Christianity Today*'s fiftieth anniversary web page.

CAN AN UNFEELING GOD LOVE?

A theology that embraces the idea that God cannot suffer has to answer the question: Can God love? Abraham Heschel rightly said that the essence of Hebraic prophetic faith is that God takes the people of his covenantal love so seriously that he suffers for their actions. God "indwells" the Israelites so that he even goes with them into Babylonian exile and feels their sorrowful plight. This capacity to feel for the other in vulnerable love is part of what it means to be God.

If love implies vulnerability, the traditional understanding of God as impassible makes it impossible to say that "God is love." An almighty God who cannot suffer is poverty stricken because he cannot love or be involved. If God remains unmoved by whatever we do, there is really very little point in doing one thing rather than the other. If friendship means allowing oneself to be affected by another, then this unmoved, unfeeling deity can have no friends or be our friend.

Elie Wiesel, Jewish survivor of the Holocaust, never shrinks from saying that the opposite of love is not hatred but indifference. If God were indifferent, he could not love. This is made plain in Wiesel's story about the hanging of two Jewish men and a youth in a Nazi concentration camp. All the prisoners, Wiesel included, were paraded before the gallows to witness this horrifying spectacle. "The men died quickly, but the death throes of the youth lasted for half an hour. 'Where is God? Where is he?' someone asked behind me. As the youth still hung in torment in the noose after a long time, I heard the man call again, 'Where is God?' And I heard a voice in myself answer: 'Where is he? He is here. He is hanging there on the gallows.'" Any other answer would be blasphemy, says Jurgen Moltmann.

God suffers because God wills to love. When I was eight years old, I lost my father to cancer. A week after his burial, I became severely ill. The pain in my body eventually paralyzed me. I still remember how my mother, newly widowed, cared for me. She did not discuss with me how I felt. Instinctively she took me into her arms and caressed my back with her gentle hands, reassuring me with words of comfort and love for me. I grew so sick that I was hospitalized. Since we lived in a remote village about ten miles from the hospital, my mother carried me there on her back, walking powerfully, uphill and down. With tears streaming down her cheek, she said: "Son, Daddy is not here. But Mommy is still here. Hang in there. We will make it to the hospital soon."

This childhood experience confirmed for me that a love that does not suffer with the suffering of the beloved is not love at all. What consolation would it have been if my mother had remained aloof from my suffering? Of what help to wounded people is a God who knows nothing of pain himself? "Only the suffering God can help," Dietrich Bonhoeffer wrote from his death cell. God helps not through supernatural miracles, but through his own wounds—his suffering with victims and sufferers.

Our Christian foreparents were right to speak of God as impassible if that means God is not emotionally unstable and cannot be manipulated by humans. But they were wrong to conclude from this that God has no passion. They were wrong to think a suffering God is an imperfect being who necessarily seeks his perfection and tries to overcome his deficiency though actions. C. S. Lewis makes a helpful distinction between "gift love" (*agape*) and "need love" (*eros*). God does not act out of need love—a love dominated by self-seeking desires. Rather, God acts out of gift love—a free, self-giving love—sharing his boundless goodness without thought of return. God's goodness means that he loves us with a completely unconditional love, involving himself with us even in our pain.

If God is devoid of passions, we would have to rewrite the Bible. The Bible eloquently affirms that God can be wounded. In Hosea, for instance, God cries out about wayward Israel: "How can I give you up, Ephraim? How can I hand you over, O Israel? My heart recoils within me; my compassion grows warm and tender. I will not execute my fierce anger; I will not again destroy Ephraim; for I am God and no mortal, the Holy One in your midst, and I will not come in wrath" (11:8–9, NRSV).

God suffered the pain of the broken relationship with Israel, but as the Japanese scholar Kazoh Kitamori comments, "The 'pain' of God reflects his will to love the object of his wrath." God's anger is not a childish loss of temper nor is it a frustrated love turned sour or vindictive. Rather, it is an expression of pure love that does not allow him to stand by idly in the face of unrighteousness. God's true nature is active love; wrath is God's "strange work," which opposes anything that stands between God and us. Wrath is God's love burning hot in the presence of sin, proof that he cares.

WAS GOD PRESENT AT THE CROSS?

If the attribute of impassibility is ascribed to God, there can be no real incarnation of God in Jesus. If God is denied suffering, then the Cross cannot be a genuine revelation of God. The Greek idea of God obscured the fullness of God's self-revelation in Jesus. One result was that the early church fathers concluded that Jesus suffered in his humanity, not in his divinity; and they separated Jesus' humanity from his deity, thus in effect making each nature an independent person, as the Nestorian heresy does, thereby jeopardizing the unity of Christ. To say that the Son of God, as divine, is impassible is to affirm that Christ's divinity is untouched by the suffering of his humanity. Consequently there is no real Incarnation; or if there is, it is robbed of its main significance.

But God has willed that we should think of Jesus when we think about him. For God is revealed to us in the person of Jesus rather than through philosophy. Evangelicals should not be offended at the thought that the death of the crucified Christ involved not only the humanity of Jesus but also his deity.

As John Austin Baker says, "The crucified Jesus is the only accurate picture of God the world has ever seen." The sight of Jesus on the cross disclosed God as one who suffers with humanity. If we take the Trinity and Incarnation seriously and recognize that this human Jesus is the second divine person, there is no suffering closer to God than the suffering of the human Jesus. Thus, the human suffering of Jesus is really God's own suffering: God suffered as we do.

Further, if God is denied suffering, the Cross is evacuated of Christ's deity. Consequently, we have no salvation through him. Christ's death would be the death of just another human being, not the death of the Son of God. And his work would be merely a human work. On this delicate topic, the Lutheran theologians of *Formula of Concord* quoted Luther as saying, "Unless God is on the balance and throws his weight as a counterbalance, we shall sink to the bottom of the scale . . . . If it is not true that God died for us, but only a man died, we are lost. But if God's death and God lie dead in the opposite scale, then his side goes down and we go upward like a light or empty pan. But he could not have sat in the pan unless he became a man like us, so that it could be said, God dead, God's passion, God's blood, God's death."

Here is no surrogate; God himself died a real death, and the outcome—our salvation—hung in the balance. The greatest marvel of the gospel is that the divinity was present in the Cross, working out our salvation through the suffering of Christ. God has suffered our sin and his own wrath, thereby defeating sin. Johann Rist's Good Friday hymn echoes this:

O great distress, God himself lies dead,
he died upon the cross,
in this he won the kingdom of heaven
for love of us.

If it were true that only Christ's humanity suffered and his divinity had no part in the action of his passion, then he is of no more use to us than any other saint because his death was merely a human death. In order for God to redeem humanity from the power of death, his act must be at one and the same time a human and a divine act. God had to suffer and die in Christ. God let himself be overtaken by death in the suffering and dying of Christ, and yet he remained the victor over death.

Unlike Calvin and his followers, Luther proclaims a Christ in whom the divinity did suffer. The Reformed tradition should listen to Luther, who affirms that if God cannot really experience crucifixion, then "Christ would be too weak a savior."

The God who is known in Christ is the God who came in lowliness and humility, not in power and majesty. Christ emptied himself, not of his divinity, but of the "divine form" by assuming a "servant form" (Phil 2:5–11). He took the form of a servant, yet he remained divine. He did not withdraw his deity from the cross, but he did not use his divine power to protect himself. God in Christ experienced a public humiliation, abandoning all self-protection and self-defense in order to save us. God's *self* was poured out for us and for our salvation.

If it were not the very God himself who became sin and suffered for us, what hope of life is left? What God cannot participate in, he cannot redeem. If God has not entered into our suffering and death, then there is no hope for redemption of our pain.

HOW THEN SHOULD WE LIVE?

What are the implications of recognizing this vulnerable God as the Christian God?

The church and the Christian life should be patterned after the Cross. Just as the way of Christ was through a cross, Christ's followers must also experience the darkness and suffering of the cross. As Luther wrote graphically, "If you are a lily and rose of Christ, therefore, know that you will live among thorns."

The world must observe that we suffer not because of public scandal or vice, but because we hold to the Word of God, preach it, and practice it. In suffering we are conformed to the image of Christ.

God's loving vulnerability thus provides us with a model for Christian living in this world. Being vulnerable necessarily involves risk, pain, and loss. Acts 9 tells how Ananias, in obedience to the Lord's vision, risked his reputation to seek out Saul, the enemy of the Christian faith; and then the whole Damascus church, in love and obedience, risked its security by forgiving Saul's violent past and welcoming him into the church.

This is what it means to make love our first priority. "Where the world exploits, [the Christian] will dispossess himself, and where the world oppresses, he will stoop down and raise up the oppressed. If the world refuses justice, the Christian will pursue mercy, and if the world takes refuge in lies, he will open his mouth for the dumb, and bear testimony to the truth . . . [on behalf of] Jew or Greek, bond or free, strong or weak, noble or base" (Bonhoeffer).

My neighbor, an arrogant and wealthy businessman, scorned the church for many years. Whenever church members phoned him, he would criticize them: "You church people are only interested in my money. You don't care for me; you only care about my pocketbook." But then he became ill and was paralyzed. When I went to visit him, to my utter surprise his entire room looked like a flower shop, and cards were posted everywhere on the wall. The flowers and cards came from church members whom he so disdained for many years. Posted on the wall, facing his bed, was a big sheet of paper with these words on it: "I was wrong. The church does care." Later he became a Christian, all because of the church's willingness to risk loving vulnerability.

The church of the suffering God must exist in and for this world, accepting suffering itself as it cares for the needy, the sick, and the poor and seeks the liberation of the oppressed. If God is found in the human suffering of Jesus, we should not then preach a triumphalist doctrine of health, wealth, and freedom from affliction for those who believe.

Once a Christian couple came to me in Russia, requesting that I pray for divine healing for their sick baby. After prayer, the baby died in my arms. One could have asked, "Where is God?" Triumphalism has nothing to say at such moments, except lashing the wounded into deeper guilt and pain for their supposed lack of faith. But these bereaved parents said, "It is better to be in the storm with Jesus than to be in it without Jesus."

The belief in a suffering God can provide an appropriate entry point for sharing the gospel. A few years ago, I was in the former Czechoslovakia on a preaching tour. On the plane home a government official spoke to me. He told me that he had attended the service when I had spoken about Christ's suffering for his people, and he had left the service in rage, cursing God for the suffering he and his family had known: forty years of suffering under Communist rule; the starvation and death of his parents; the long years he had spent as a lonely child in an orphanage.

His rage continued when he arrived home. On the apartment wall hung a crucifix, given to him by his mother with the prayer that one day he would come to Christ. Furious, he hurled a cake topped with thick, white icing at it. The icing covered the crucifix, dripping down the face of the crucified figure. And in that moment, my words about Christ's suffering came alive to him. For the first time, he said, he saw Jesus' tears. In his apartment, he knelt in front of the cross and gave his life to Christ. And he uttered these words: "Christ is for me, not against me."

The man told me: "I don't understand many of the things that happened politically, but I know that Jesus did not forsake me. He was in pain when I was in pain. He was in tears when I was in tears. He did not experience joy when I suffered the most." Forgoing speculation as to why suffering befell him, he was now risking himself to the loving care of the Divine Sufferer. It sufficed this wounded governor to perceive in the Cross God's deepest pain and his loving scars. Thus sensing God's presence in his suffering, it enabled him to receive the gospel, and eventually to find faith.

Our compassionate God meets us in every corner of our lives. Catherine of Siena once cried out: "My God and Lord, where were you when my heart was plunged in darkness and filth?" And she heard a voice: "My daughter, did you feel it? I was in your heart." Because our Lord knows pain firsthand, we can pray with confidence that he will be moved by our cries.

How our prayers are answered is a matter of God's wisdom and sovereignty, and to these we may well submit with the assurance that he hugs us close to him as his beloved.

In turmoil and trials, Staupitz's pastoral advice to Luther speaks to us, too: "Contemplate the wounds of Christ and the blood that was shed for you." With this we can be assured in our hearts, "I am his, and he is mine! He was in agony for us on the cross; he feels for me and with me still; *he cares!*" And that, surely, is the best news ever.

3

Three Undeniable Realities: Altars, Prisons, and Cemeteries[*]

IN EVERY CIVILIZATION, ANCIENT and modern, and in every country, East, West, North, and South, one will be able to observe three things: altars, prisons, and cemeteries. These are not there simply for us to see or talk about; rather, they speak to us of the three undeniable realities of human life and experience. And yet the Gospel can shed light on them, and is the remedy for what each of them represents. Let me offer a Christian response to these empirical realities.

Altars: Religiosity and Piety

First, altars tell us that we, as God's creatures, are essentially religious, as we are created to be. As one anthropologist said, "[a] human being is incurably religious." God-consciousness is part of what constitutes a religious being. We are aware of God quite apart from any philosophical arguments. This is why the Bible never attempts to prove God, but simply declares that God is. As sufficient proof, Genesis 1:1 affirms, "In the beginning, God created the heavens and the earth." Psalm 19:1 declares, "The heavens declare the glory of God; the skies proclaim the work of his hands." While Psalm 14:1 says, "The fool says in his heart, 'there is no God.'" In Romans 1:19–20, Paul wrote, "What may be known about God is plain to them. For since the creation of the world God's invisible qualities—his eternal power and divine nature—have been clearly seen, being understood from what has been made, so that men are without excuse."

---

* With variations, this apologetic sermon was delivered in 1993 at First Alliance Church of Scarborough, Canada, where I served as Preaching Associate under the tutelage of the Rev. Dr. Ross Ingram, the *Centre's* Senior Churchman award recipient (2005).

The sparkling stars in the sky and the speaking conscience within us lend support to the existence of the Creator God.

To be created in the image of God is to be endowed with a seed of religion, which Calvin calls *divinitatis sensus*, a sense of the divinity.[1] God has not only implanted in all people a certain understanding of his existence, but also discloses himself daily in the splendorous workmanship of his universe. So clear and so prominent is God's self-disclosure that none can take refuge in the pretense of ignorance. This innate knowledge of God is set within us, and God repeatedly renews it by shedding fresh drops of his richest manifestations in nature and providence. The enhanced knowledge of God revealed in nature serves to strengthen the faith of believers. Calvin wrote, "Therefore it was his will that the history of creation be made manifest, in order that the faith of the church, resting upon this, might seek no other God but him who was put forth by Moses as the Maker and Founder of this universe."[2]

Faith affirms God as the origin and goal of all that is. This knowledge sheds light on who God is in relation to us, which he is the giver of all, and simultaneously illumines who we are in relation to him, the recipients of all his gifts. Thus familiarity with one's self and an understanding of God is mutually connected. The knowledge of God, the Creator in Scripture, corresponds to that gained from the imprint, which shines in his creatures; both have worship as their intended goal. Scripture invites us first to revere God, then trust in him then finally, through these things, we learn to worship him. This knowledge of God (the Father) as the fountainhead and source of all good begets a piety fused with an earnest fear of God, a fear that results in voluntary reverence and true service or worship. God constitutes his creatures in such a way that they naturally possess a knowledge of him that leads them to revere the origin of the good they experience. There resides in all an intrinsic unity of knowledge of God and worship that they may aspire to revere and worship his majesty and make him the sole goal of all their actions. This is intimated in Calvin's commentary on Malachi 1:11, "We must bear in mind that God cannot rightly be worshipped except he is known."[3]

1. John Calvin, *Institutes of the Christian Religion*, 1.3.1. Edited by John T. McNeil. Translated by Ford Lewis Battles. Philadelphia: Westminster, 1960.
2. Ibid., 1.14.1.
3. Cited in Witvliet, *Worship Seeking Understanding*, 152.

Three Undeniable Realities: Altars, Prisons, and Cemeteries

The spiritual nature in human beings propels them to set up altars to express their devotion with. Human beings cannot help but worship, even if the object of worship may be wrong. When man does not have a god, he will certainly have an idol. Why? Because he is so constituted that he must set his religious affections on something or someone. This was what happened to the Romans who exchanged the glory of the immortal God for graven images, and thus worshipped and served created things rather than the Creator. Even a non-Christian professor of philosophy, whom I came to know, recognizes this as a given fact, and does so with conviction. He spoke thus to a group of seekers,

> All of us sitting here in this class have a sense of what it means to be religiously pious. When religiosity and piety are turned Godward, man begins to glorify God, and worship God as God. On the contrary, when religiosity and piety are turned inward to the self, man will inevitably dethrone the God of the universe, but enthrone the self as God. He then begins to worship himself as God. When the self becomes its own God, universal madness and inhumanity will break out.

After a successful ministry, I took a walk down a narrow street. I was holding a black Bible and singing a familiar song: "The Lord knows the way through the wilderness. All I have to do is to follow." I saw a tall, middle-aged man staring at me as I walked past him. The next morning, a newspaper headline read, "Murders and Rapes," along with a picture of the man I had seen the previous night. Rather angry, I phoned up some friends who got me connected with the prison where the criminal was being kept. When I saw him, he was quite surprised.

I asked, "You saw me passing by you last night?"

He said, "Yes, I recognize you. You were the preacher with the black Bible."

I asked, "So, you believe in God?"

He said, "Yes, I used to believe in your God. But ten years ago, I killed him. I have decided to be God myself; I am my own God."

I asked him: "Does your killing of my God make you sad or glad?"

His reply was disturbing: "I don't have any feelings at all. Why talk about feeling sad or mad? I have chosen hell to be an eternal dwelling."

When the self is worshipped as God, inhumanity occurs. The philosopher Nietzsche was right to prophesy that when God was killed, people started killing each other. And the twentieth century marked the bloodiest century yet. The apostle Paul reasoned in Romans 1:21ff. that when men rejected God as God, their thinking became futile, their foolish hearts were darkened, and their will became bent toward evil. Because God, the foundation of life, had been removed, they became senseless, faithless, heartless, hopeless, and ruthless.

Friends, what are we to do with the religious instinct within us? God implants it there so that we might turn to him and worship him, the one worthy of our praise. A Russian Christian remarked that communism can kill us, but not God, for he is forever alive in the depths of our souls. No matter what circumstances befall, St. Augustine's words still ring true, "Our heart is restless until it finds rest in God."[4] This also finds support in Psalm 42:1–2, where the Psalmist cried, "My soul thirsts for God, the living God. As the deer pants for stream of water, so my soul pants for you, O God."

Prison: Total Depravity and Imprisonment

Secondly, prisons tell us about the negative side of human nature, which is totally depraved and is thus in need of healing. Prisons bear witness to the imprisonment of our nature by sin. The systemic problem we face is sin, and the symptoms are sinful deeds. St. Paul wrote in Romans 3:10, "There is no one righteous, not even one." Consequently the seed of religion, which is ontologically constitutive of our creaturely status, seldom takes root, and when it does, it tends to achieve the opposite of God's original intention (worship). Instead of leading us upward to God, it leads us downward to death, blindness, and spiritual destruction. Scarcely anyone actuates this inclination toward God and the one who does fosters it in a distorted manner, bearing dangerous and deformed fruits. The sinner can only respond to this desire erroneously, either by suppressing its effects or by perverting its intended purpose.

All of us are sinners, without exception, without escape, and without excuse. G. K. Chesterston once asserted, "The doctrine of original sin is the one philosophy empirically validated by thirty-five hundred years of human history."[5] A painter was painting a person, whose T-shirt has this

---

4. See 1.1.1 in *Augustine's Confessions*, 3. Translated by Henry Chadwick. Oxford: Oxford University Press, 1991.

5. Quoted in Roy B. Zuck, *The Speaker's Quote Book*, 350. Grand Rapids, MI: Kregel, 1997.

sentence "I am an angel." He painted him ugly, and he changed the original sentence to "I am a *fallen* angel." That person was upset, and refused to pay the bill. The painter was perceptive about the human condition. Undeniably we are a *fallen* angel, even when we may look like an angel, or be considered as one.

Sin manifests itself in different ways or forms. We sin in our pretense. We pretend to do good so as to earn righteousness before God, but we do not know what it means to be godly. We try to be philosophers, thinking up answers to our questions, and in the process become puffed up. We try to be philosophers when we do not know the Master Philosopher, the divine Wisdom. We try to portray an artistic perception of the beauty of God's handiwork, yet we have no intimate relationship with the one who is the source of all that is. We sin by beautifying the beast and demonizing the beauty. We sin by making the absolute relative and making the relative absolute. We sin by making the infinite finite and making the finite infinite. We sin by calling good evil and calling evil good. We sin by closing ourselves to the goodness of God while opening ourselves to the evil of the world. We sin by paying lip service to the Most High, yet the Most High is kept at a distance from us. We sin in our hidden desire to be God, accountable to no one.

The essence of sin is our refusal to accept our creaturely status and divine Creatorship. This refusal results in a usurpation of divine authority, or an autonomy of self. Despite these sinful tendencies and acts, God still pours out his love upon sinners, "God demonstrates his love in that while we are still sinners, Christ died for us (Rom 5:8)". When faced with the burdensome reality of guilt and sin, there is still the soothing reality of liberation and forgiveness. Over against the reality of prison, there is the greater reality of the cross. The love of God is so great that it loves miserable sinners like us. Who amongst us has not sinned? And yet who amongst us has sins so great that they cannot be forgiven? D. L. Moody wrote, "God has cast out confessed sins into the depths of the sea, and he even put a 'no fishing' sign over the spot."[6] "As far as the east is from the west, so far has God removed our transgressions from us" (Ps 103:12). Thus, there is no need for us to punish ourselves for past sins, or condemn ourselves into the prison of sin again. It is folly for people to punish them-

6. Quoted in Albert Wells, *Inspiring Quotations. Contemporary & Classical*, 80. Nashville: Thomas Nelson, 1988.

selves when their sins are already forgiven. We should heed the Spirit's wooing when he said, "Wilt thou be clean?"

Ernest Hemingway told a story of a boy named Paco in Spain. His relationship with his father was broken. Subsequently, Paco left home and became a prodigal son. His father grieved over this broken relationship, but was earnestly seeking for his son. So he put an advertisement in the newspaper, "Paco, my son, please meet me tomorrow at noon in front of the town courthouse. All is forgotten." Interestingly enough, Paco is a very common name in Spain. The next day, more than five hundred boys by the same name appeared in the designated place—all of them wanted forgiveness.

Are we not the same? There are no exceptions in this, for we too desire a fresh beginning, a new chapter. The phrase "all is forgotten" is indeed a sweet sound to the ears and a deep consolation to wayward hearts, causing them to return and appropriate the gift of forgiveness.

The cross is where God's "yes" to sinners is spoken, the consoling and efficacious voice, which issues forth repentance in sinners' hearts. An indescribable joy emanates from the liberating work of the cross. The cross bears witness to the love of God, who suffers for sin, and defeats it for those who believe. It reveals how great God's love is towards us, and correspondingly how priceless we are in God's sight. Augustine said, "God loves us as though but one worthy of his love."[7] We are worth the precious blood of Jesus Christ. And St. John declared, "How great is the love the Father has lavished on us, that we should be called the children of God! And this is what we are!" (1 John 3:1).

Cemeteries: Death and Decay

Cemeteries tell us about the grim reality of death. They speak so powerfully that we are brought face to face with the undeniable facts of decay and death. No one can deny, excuse, or escape it. Cemeteries, mostly located away from the noisy and busy city, can be a place for quiet solemn meditation on death. We must observe the proper timing for contemplating death. The might of death becomes increasingly greater and fear of it becomes more intense because of our lack of timely contemplation. During our lifetime, we should invite death into our consciousness when it is still at a distance. At the last hour, we should banish all thoughts of

7. Wells, *Inspiring Quotations*, 80.

death, but meditate upon life at that moment. Death is the one evil, which the Bible ascribes fear to. People would rather choose to submit to all other evils, if they could thereby avoid the evil of death. Even the saints dreaded it, and Christ submitted to it with trembling fear and bloody sweat (Luke 22:42–44). Therefore, in no other area has God's mercy been more concerned with consoling faint hearts than in the matter of death.

There was a Broadway Musical entitled, *A Little Night*. In it, there was a party. There the grandmother stood to propose a toast, and it was a toast to life. Everybody quickly and joyfully joined in all at once, thrilled at the possibility of life. But the grandmother went on to propose another toast. She said to the people in the party, "let us now give a toast to the other great reality, a toast to death." There was complete silence in the party. Sadness and fury filled the hearts of the people there.

If I were there, I would have felt more mad than sad at the grandmother who could talk of death so lightly and happily? It is unnatural and irrational to talk of death as if it were our friend. It is unreasonable to toast death, for the Bible said, "Death is the last enemy." Death is the enemy to our love, our family, our romance, our accomplishment or labor, and to everything we hold dear. This explains why many people spend all their lives banishing all thoughts of death, the very enemy and antithesis of life.

Christianity does not deny the grim reality of death, "Death came upon all mankind because of sin" (Rom 5:12). But over against the reality of death, there is a glorious affirmation of Jesus Christ who claimed, "I am the resurrection and the life. Whoever believes in me will live forever, even though he dies" (John 11:25–26). All fears are annihilated because of the power of Jesus' resurrection. Michael Green said it well, "Jesus' resurrection from the death at the first Easter marks the day when death died." Thus, the greatest funeral of all is that of death, not that of you and me. Death has been swallowed up, and so buried that it shall never assail us or hold us in captivity. The resurrection of Jesus Christ is the greatest blessing and where the believer finds his supreme joy and lasting possessions. The risen Christ killed death by his death and restored life by his resurrection so that in him there is not the slightest sign of evil, but only good.

Those who are plagued by the fear of impending death should contemplate death not in themselves, nor in their nature, nor in those who died by divine wrath and were overcome by death, in which case they were lost. Instead they should contemplate death only in those who die in God's grace, and in Christ, who overcame death with life. The more they fix their gazes upon Christ, the more Christ glows. Consequently death becomes contemptible and dead, slain and overcome in life. As Luther said, "For Christ is nothing other than sheer life, as his saints are likewise."[8] Christ's death is the chief object of meditation, for he is the dead bronze serpent in whose sight the agents and might of death die. Christ takes our death upon him and strangles it so that it no longer harms us, if we believe that he does it for us and see our death in him and not in us. Thus to look at death in any other way will annihilate us with terror and anguish.

In some places, cemetery and church are right next to each other. This juxtaposition is of theological importance, while cemeteries speak to us about the fact of death, the terrifying enemy, churches proclaim the fact of future resurrection, this terrific news. Whoever believes and lives in Christ are members of the people of hope and of future resurrection. Thus we can tell the world that the way out of the grave is to be united with the risen Christ. All of us, the living in churches and the dead in church-yards, are awaiting the day when there will be a great reunion of the saints in heaven. People in the cemeteries will be resurrected, transformed, and transferred to the celestial heaven where there will be no pain, no sorrow, no tears, no fears, no darkness, and no sickness; every imperfection and separation will be wiped out. This is why those who believe in Christ have got nothing to lose, but everything to gain.

There was an inscription on a tombstone:

> Pause when you pass me by.
> Where you are now, so was I;
> Where I am now, so will you.
> Be prepared and follow me.

As a reply, somebody wrote underneath it:

> To follow you I am not content,
> unless you tell me which way you went—heaven or hell.

Jesus said, "I am the Way to heaven." And St. Paul wrote, "For me to live is Christ; to die is gain" (Phil 1:21). For in Christ we have all we need. Faith relies on him totally for good, and flees to him in every hour of need. And that is the greatest news!

---

8. Cited in Ngien, *Luther as a Spiritual Adviser*, 34. Bletchley: Paternoster, 2007.

4

T. H. I. N. K:
Grieve Not the Holy Spirit*
(Ephesians 4:29–32)

I HEARD A GRADUATION address that was remarkably salient and profound. Facing the graduating class, the speaker said,

> Dear graduates, I know all of you are well-equipped with the skills
> and training with which to serve your country. Many of you would
> have no problem in doing well in society, but only those who are
> skilful in the use of their tongues will do better. What is true hap-
> piness? True happiness is found in more than achieving a degree.
> Rather it is in one's ability to use their tongue wisely so as to im-
> pute dignity and worth into the lives of others.

It has been said that every part of our physical body will soon be worn out, like an old pair of shoes, all except our tongue. No matter how old we may be, our tongue always remains young and sharp. The tongue is indeed a very helpful tool. But when it is misused or abused, it can become a lethal poison. This explains why Paul warned us in Ephesians 4:29, "Do not let any unwholesome talk come out of your mouth, but only what is helpful for building others up according to their needs." In other words, stop all unproductive speech; only say good things, things that are edifying.

Interestingly enough, immediately after speaking about human speech and the tongue, Paul proceeded to write about grieving the Holy Spirit. Verse 30 reads, "Do not grieve the Holy Spirit by which you are sealed for the day of redemption." There seems to be a close connection between verses 29 and 30. The juxtaposition of unwholesome speech (v. 29) and grieving the Holy Spirit (v. 30) is significant, implying that we

---

* This sermon was preached 2001 at the Youth Spiritual Convention of Methodist Church in Malaysia.

may grieve the Spirit by our wrong actions or speech. All three persons of the Trinity, each singly God, are altogether one God, and thus they equally share the same attributes. Like the Father and the Son, the Spirit possesses characteristics such as intelligence, will and emotions. In this context, the Spirit can be grieved or saddened by our unwholesome talk, through the abuse and misuse of our tongue and language. If we have a critical spirit, we might bring sadness to the person of the Spirit, by which we are sealed for the day of redemption.

All of us—young and old—are critical at times. Even small children criticize. Children have a way of going straight to you and telling you like it is. When he was drinking a glass of milk, my four-year-old Hansel turned his head towards me and criticized, "Dad, don't preach so loud." I asked, "Hansel, how should I do it?" He replied, "Ask mommy; she will teach you how." Another time, I was dressed in a virgin blue shirt given to me by an aunt. My boy spotted it and said with disapproval, "Dad, blue is not your color. Return it to aunty; get another one from her." Have not all parents been embarrassed by their dear little ones? And by the time they are teenagers, they are pros at it. This reminds me of a bumper sticker I saw, which reads as follows, "I can handle any critics. I have children at home." How true this is!

"Criticism," says Aristotle, "is something you can avoid easily, by saying nothing, doing nothing and being nothing."[1] There is some truth to what he said. However, Aristotle's statement is of course unrealistic, for we will inevitably say something, do something and be someone. To be sure, this consubstantial triad—speaking, doing, and being—creates the risk of being criticized. For example, before I became a father, no one criticized me for doing a bad job of it. But as soon as I became one, I start receiving criticism. Likewise, the moment I stepped into the pulpit, people began criticizing my preaching, sometimes vehemently. Therefore, to say that one could avoid criticism completely is a utopian proposition. Criticism is unavoidable, and comes from being part of the human family or, rather, the fallen human family.

It can be very difficult for us to handle, sometimes necessary, but probably never wanted. Suppose we do need to give criticism, how could we do it in a way that would not grieve the Holy Spirit, and will also not grieve each other unnecessarily? How can we run a committee meeting

1 Quoted in Zuck, *The Speaker's Quote Book*, 94.

without grieving the Holy Spirit? Let me offer a formula, a guiding principle, think before you lash out. The five-letter word—T - H - I - N - K—forms a basis for our reflection.

The Truthfulness of the Information

The letter "T" touches on the question, "Is it true?" This concerns the status of the information we gather. Is our perception reliable? Is the information true? Did you hear it from others and simply believe it without checking its veracity? Or perhaps you have exaggerated what you heard. We need to be aware that people tend to believe the negative more readily than the positive. Negative news is easily and quickly blown out of proportion. The following story is illustrative of this.

> A pastor leaned over and told his colleague: 'John, my ear kind of hurts today. Please pray for me.' The front pew overheard the pastor, and one leaned over to the other and said, 'The pastor has an ear ache, which calls for prayer.' However the people behind them heard it differently: 'Pastor has a hearing aid [mistaken for ear ache].' Next, those a few pews behind them said, 'Pastor is having trouble hearing today.' However, the people further back said, 'Pastor is wearing a double-earring [mistaken for trouble hearing] today.' Finally, in exasperation, the last few members remarked: 'That's it. I am getting out of this church if the pastor is wearing a double-earring.

Check things out before anybody leaves the church. Make sure of the status of information so that we do not jump to conclusions, and thus grieve the Holy Spirit.

The Pain of Criticism

The letter "H" deals with the question: Does it hurt me to criticize? This concerns your motive, or what we could call the heart condition. The best way to check your motive is to ask the question, does it bring me pain or pleasure when I criticize? Does it hurt you to do it? If you get a lot of enjoyment out of criticizing someone, it may be that this suggests some problems in your life. But if it brings you a lot of pain or sleepless nights and you wish you did not have to do it, if you do not delight in doing it but feel that you should say something, then your motive is probably right and pure. Paul writes in verse 31, "Get rid of all bitterness, rage, brawling and slander, along with every form of malice." Are our hearts infected with these vices? Do we speak out of a heart dominated by these germs? If so, we sadden the Holy Spirit. Those who hear our critical comments will not be built up.

The Consequence of Criticism

The letter "I" relates to the question, "Is it inspiring?" This is about the outcome of our criticism. We were exhorted to speak in a manner that would "benefit those who listen" (v. 29). Does my criticism inspire the hearer to grow and glow, to do better and become a lovely person? Is there something I could share that would encourage godlikeness in them? Unfortunately, some people criticize not to inspire but to insult, to humiliate, and to make people feel small, ugly, and incompetent. The end result is shame and degradation. It could happen in a marriage. Imagine a husband saying, "Honey, now that we are married . . . do you mind if I point out some of your defects?" His beloved may well reply, "Dear, not at all. But you should know this, it is those defects that keep me from getting a better husband." His criticism does not inspire romance; romance can disappear like the wind. Are we inspiring our staff, our children, or our spouse to reach their maximum potential? Often our criticism limits, rather than increases, the potential of others.

The Severity of the Issue

The letter "N" raises the question, of necessity. This deals with the severity of the issue. Is it really necessary that I bring it out? Is it a genuinely important issue? Do I have to speak out or can I keep quiet, even if there is some truth to the criticism? Maybe it is not a vital issue. It might be our own pettiness that prompts us to criticize. Paul says in verse 31, "Get rid of brawling." Brawlers are the compulsive and natural critics who sharpen their tongues like piercing swords and shoot bitter words like deadly arrows (cf. Ps 64:3). They are contentious, noisy, and onerous. Some have rightly put it like this, oftentimes it is not so much the size of the issue but the size of our heart that causes us to criticize. God forbids that we should be so small-minded, wrangling over things that have little or no importance. Joe Belz illustrates the discipline of a good tongue through an analogy with a plumber, "Any faucet can turn the water on, but only a good one will turn it off."

There is an inherent danger in criticism, however constructive it may be. Floyd Goins's comment is worth noting, "I realize how dangerous criticism can be, even when we try to sanctify the term by calling it constructive criticism. It is often tainted with personal feelings and reactions." In addition, it is thought to take at least ten positive comments to offset one negative comment. Therefore, if you do not have to criticize, do not do it. Turn the faucet of criticism off. It takes no brilliance to find faults, but it is brilliance to find solutions. Do not just come to people with critical comments, but come with creative solutions. If you cannot find creative solutions, then it is not necessary to give, however important we may feel it is.

The Attitude of Criticism

The letter "K" deals with the question: "Am I kind?" This concerns our personal attitude, the spirit in which we give criticism. Verse 32 reads, "Be kind to each other, be compassionate and forgive each other as God has forgiven us in Christ." If criticism is offered in kindness, others will receive it with kindness. We need to ask ourselves, am I kind, sympathetic, and forgiving when I point out the wrongs or weaknesses in others? Or do I do it out of bitterness, rage, and slander, along with every form of malice? If we do it in kindness, compassion, and forgiveness, it could be a vital stimulus for self-examination and personal growth. Otherwise, it may lead to depreciation,

This is the area where most of us fail, including me. I recall that years ago a kind but wearied mother complained to me, "Pastor Dennis, my son would have turned out alright, if you as his pastor had paid a little more attention to his personal feelings." Her criticism cut deep, and came with conviction to me, as it was from a mother who was deeply worried about her son. Her son was rebellious; he often read newspapers or something other than the Bible in services, especially during preaching. I used to be very harsh on teenagers, forgetting I was once just like them, if not worse. I repented before God, pleading earnestly for this teenager not to stray from God because of my attitude. Praise God that he returned to God and is now serving in the youth ministry. So we must look at ourselves before lashing out at others. This will temper us into kindness, compassion, and forgiveness because we know how deep we have fallen.

My old and feeble mother used to call me "baby." In fact, she still does and I enjoy it. I remember an incident that happened when I was twelve years old. Mom and I had a conflict over some trivial matter. I lost my temper. I screamed at her disrespectfully and criticized her unfairly in front of others in the family. I still remember, as vividly as if it were yesterday, that she came to me, putting both her hands on my shoulder, and grinned at me. Oh! The mother's grin is so convicting and unbearable. She said this, "Go and find my baby." I cried, "I am your baby." But she insisted, "You are not the real baby. Find yourself and we will talk." This philosophical insight from a woman who had had only a grade one education has remained with me ever since. She could have lectured and corrected me publicly, but she did not. Her kindness, compassion, and forgiving spirit have touched my inner being.

To be kind is to communicate worth and bring wholeness to others; to be compassionate is to feel the hurt and bring healing to the wounded; and to forgive is to liberate the wrong-doers from the burden of guilt, and set the wounded free from bitter rage that so easily destroys a seemingly good relationship.

Let us heed the biblical exhortation, "Hark our tongues! Grieve not the Holy Spirit!" Let us learn to think before criticizing.

5

Learning Preaching from a Hero of Faith*

INTRODUCTION

The preaching office constitutes a sure sign of a true church. Wherever the word of God is preached, said Luther, there is no doubt Christian people are there, even though their number may be small. It is supremely through the words of the preacher that the Word of God in the Scriptures is made alive in the present. He wrote, "One must see the word of the preacher as God's Word."[1] He then elaborated on this, "The apostles wrote very little, but they spoke a lot. Notice, it says let their voices be heard; not let their books be read. The ministry of the New Testament is not engraved on dead tablets of stone; rather it sounds in a living voice. Through a living Word God accomplishes and fulfills his gospel."[2] Thus the church is not a "pen house," but a "mouth house."[3] The gospel, which is hidden in the Scriptures, must be preached and performed by word of mouth and a living voice.

Preaching has a dual nature: divine and human by means of God's Word through human speech. It is an indispensable means of grace, and is central to church liturgy. This chapter focuses on four major aspects that elucidate the theology of preaching of Martin Luther, my hero of faith:

---

* This is a shorter version of a larger article published in *Themelios* 28 (2003): 28–48.

1. LW 22, 526. The primary sources for this study is the English translation of Luther's works of the *American Editions*, vols. 1–30 edited by Jaroslav Pelikan. St. Louis: Concordia, 1955–1967. And vols. 31–55, edited by Helmut Lehman. Philadelphia: Fortress, 1955–1967. Hereafter abbreviated as *LW*. References from the *Weimar Ausgabe*, abbreviated as *WA*, will be cited where helpful.

2. See WA 5, 537 as quoted in A. Skevington Wood, *Captive to the Word*, 90. Grand Rapids, MI: Eerdmans, 1949.

3. See WA 10, I, 48 as cited in Timothy George, *Theology of the Reformers*, 91. Nashville: Broadman, 1988.

1. How his doctrine of the Word of God governs his preaching;

2. How law and gospel, both functions of one and the same Word, are to be preached;

3. How he preached Christ as sacrament and example, the appropriateness of which will be delineated;

4. How the Word and the Spirit work together in unity, fulfilling the efficacy of preaching.

The Word of God in preaching

While medieval theology developed the doctrine of the sacraments, Luther was the first to construct a doctrine of the Word of God. This doctrine permeates all of his lectures, commentaries, treatises, and sermons. The reformer, held captive by and to the Word of God, preached extensively and his sermons number over two thousand. In his *Table Talk*, he expounded on the various constituents of the term "Word,"

> Somebody asked, 'Doctor, is the Word that Christ spoke when he was on earth the same in fact and in effect as the Word preached by a minister?' The doctor replied, 'Yes, because he said, 'He who hears you hears me' (Luke 10:16). And Paul calls the Word 'the power of God' (Rom 1:16).
>
> Then the inquirer asked, 'Doctor, isn't there a difference between the Word that became flesh (John 1:14) and the Word that is proclaimed by Christ or by a minister?'
>
> 'By all means!' he replied. 'The former is the incarnate Word, who was true God from the beginning, and the latter is the Word that's proclaimed. The former Word is in substance God; the latter Word is in its effect the power of God, but isn't God in substance, for it has a man's nature, whether it's spoken by Christ or by a minister.'[4]

It is through the preached Word that God is present with his people and continues to meet them salvifically. God assumes human form in order to speak with them "as man speaks with man."[5] Just as God is to be found in his incarnate Word, he too is to be found in his preached word, which is "in its effect the power of God."

---

4. *LW* 54, 394, no. 5177.
5. *LW* 4, 61.

God has willed that we have nothing to do with him in his naked majesty, or him in so far as he is not preached or revealed. He does not wish us to search for him apart from the clothed Word, namely Christ incarnate, crucified, and resurrected from the dead. Therefore, preaching must observe the limit which God has prescribed as such,

> We have to argue in one way about God or the will of God as preached, revealed, offered, and worshipped, and in another way about God as he is not preached, not revealed, not offered, not worshipped. To the extent therefore, that God hides himself and wills to be unknown to us, it is no business of ours. For here the saying truly applies, 'Things above us are no business of ours.'[6]

Luther criticized Erasmus for failing to see the distinction between the God preached and God hidden, between the Word of God and God himself.

> God must be left to himself in his own majesty, for in this regard we have nothing to do with him, nor has he willed that we should have anything to do with him. But we have something to do with him insofar as he is clothed and set forth in his Word, through which he offers himself to us and which is the beauty and glory with which the psalmist celebrates him as being clothed.[7]

Above all, true preaching must deal with the clothed deity or incarnate Word—the Savior who was promised and figured in the Old Testament and was made incarnate in the New Testament for our salvation—for this is where God wills to be found.

It is the office of a true apostle to preach of the Passion and resurrection, and lay a foundation for faith in Christ. All preaching worthy of the name must have Jesus himself as its center and focus. With audacity, Luther identified the Word of God as the gospel. Commenting on Romans 1, Luther remarked, "The Word is the Gospel of God concerning his Son who was made flesh, suffered, rose from the dead, and was glorified through the Spirit who sanctifies."[8] The true nature of the gospel as Word was the spoken form, "The gospel is essentially proclamation, Christ coming to us through the sermons."[9] This explains why Luther insisted that

---

6. *LW* 33, 138–39.

7. Ibid.

8. *LW* 31, 176–77.

9. E. Theodore Bachman, "Introduction to volume 35," *LW* 35, xvii.

the New Testament is essentially the spoken word that it is to be preached and discussed orally with a living voice.

By the verse, "And God said: Let there be light and there was light," he understood the Word as the instrument God employed to accomplish his work of creation. The phrase "God said" means not only the utterance of God, but also the action or deed of God.[10] God's Word is causative efficaciously, speaking reality into existence in his Covenants. This understanding came from his reading of Ockham and his own study of the Psalms and Genesis in particular. The prophets speak and in their speaking the work of God is accomplished. "In the case of God to speak is to do, and the word is the deed."[11] God's Word acts and accomplishes his will. God's Word is his instrument of power, which takes created forms. Luther, following Ockham, claimed that God has chosen selected elements of his created order, which are intrinsically good, to effect his saving will. God speaks in calling into existence the created order.

In speaking through the created order, God employs the words of finite human beings to communicate with us, "For just as a man uses the tongue as a tool with which he produces and forms words, so God uses our words, whether gospel or prophetic books, as tools with which he himself writes living words in our hearts."[12] The Word of God comes to us only in the spoken form because here on earth God cannot be seen but only heard. God speaks and reveals himself "through the external word and tongue addressed to human ears."[13] Although the spoken word is that of a human being, it has been instituted by divine authority for salvation. There is a sacramental efficacy attached to the office of preaching, being when the Word of God is preached no one is exempted from its benefits. The Word of God remains free to be heard even if it comes from the mouth of Judas, Annas, Pilate, or Herod: "One should not consider who is speaking but what he is saying; for if it is the Word of God, how would God himself not be present?"[14]

Unlike the Aristotelian God, Luther's God is one who speaks with us in human language. Luther wrote, "Hear, brother: God, the creator of

10. *LW* 1, 16.
11. *LW* 12, 33.
12. *LW*, 10, 212.
13. Ibid., 10, 220.
14. Ibid., 3, 220.

heaven and earth, speaks with you through his preachers. Those words of God are not of Plato or Aristotle but God himself is speaking."[15] God must be apprehended in human speech because God so graciously wills to meet us in it. Human language, writes Peter Meinhold when discussing Luther, is seen as "a divine order in which human speech and the divine Spirit are brought together into a unity."[16] In Luther's words,

> No difference is perceptible between the word of man and the Word of God when uttered by a human being; for the voice is the same, the sound and pronunciation are the same, whether you utter divine or human words.[17]

There abides a correspondence between God hiding in his humanity to reveal himself and God hiding in human language to communicate with us. God's descent into human language is indeed God's way of relating to us, not in a foreign language but in the day-to-day language of human beings. Therefore, when we hear God's Word spoken, we should obey it wholeheartedly because God accomplishes his purpose through the ministry of human beings.

Law and Gospel: an antithetical unity

Unlike Calvinist preaching that separated the gospel from the law, Luther insisted on their antithetical unity, "When I preach a sermon I take an antithesis."[18] In other words, he never proclaims God's great "Yes" without at the same time proclaiming his terrifying "No." The law-gospel distinction does not mean a division or separation. "Nothing is more closely joined together than fear and trust, law and gospel, sin, and grace, they are so joined together that each is swallowed up by the other. Therefore there cannot be any mathematical conjunction that is similar to this." His hermeneutical distinction between law and gospel corresponds to his previous distinction between the "Letter" and the "Spirit," thus concerning two types of preaching.

> The words of the apostle, 'The letter kills, the Spirit gives life', might be said in other words, thus: 'The law kills, but the grace of God

15. *WA TR* 4, 531, no. 4812.

16. See Peter Meinhold, *Luthers Sprachphilosophie*, 13. Berlin: Lutherisches, 1958.

17. *LW* 4, 140.

18. See *WA* 36, 181 as quoted by John Doberstein, *LW* 51, xx.

gives life,' or 'Grace grants help and does everything that the law demands, and yet is unable to do it by itself.'[19]

The Word of God comes to us in two forms, as law and as gospel. God first speaks his Word of law, his alien work, which kills the sinner. Then he speaks his Word of gospel, his proper work, which recreates the sinner through the forgiveness of sins. The law as his alien work truly condemns so that we might be saved as his proper work. Law and gospel both belong to the work of the revealed God. In Luther's words: "[F]or through the law all must be humbled and through the gospel all must be exalted. They are alike in divine authority, but with respect to the fruit of ministry, they are unlike and completely opposed to each other."[20] God's assuring "Yes" is hidden in his severe "No." This double or contradictory act is done by "the same God who works everything in everyone" (1 Cor 12:6). The paradox of God's being is that God kills in order to make alive (1 Sam 2:6). The law is not against God's promises but leads people to those promises. The knowledge of a wrathful God revealed in the law is causally useful, if and when it drives us into the arms of Christ: "Thus the law was not given merely for the sake of death, but because man is proud and supposes that he is wise, righteous, and holy, therefore it is necessary that he be humbled by the law, in order that this beast, the presumption of righteousness, may be killed, since man cannot live unless it is killed."[21]

There is a preaching which is anything but saving, which works the opposite of justifying grace. Through the preaching of the law, people are made aware of the law's power, which constantly accuses them and delivers them up to God's wrath, to eternal judgment and death. This bitter truth of God's alien work must be preached, otherwise we moralize our sin, placing it in the context of our enmity to God and God's enmity to us. The deepest antithesis is not between our sin and God's grace, but between God's law and God's grace. This antithesis, so offensive to moralists, requires revelation.

Luther deplored that the sermons of his day put too much emphasis on the works of the law, turning Christ the mediator into a judge, and demanding from people righteous living. The Bielian premise, "doing what

19. Luther, 'Concerning the Letter and the Spirit,' in *Martin Luther's Basic Theological Writings*, 83. Edited by Timothy Lull. Philadelphia: Fortress, 1989.

20. *LW* 9, 178.

21. Ibid., 26, 335.

lies within us," was the presupposition of the medieval preaching. They proclaim that no one who tries to do his best will be denied grace. Only grace could save someone, but they must do something to merit it. This type of preaching precipitated in the earlier Luther a hatred of Christ.

To counteract the one sidedness of medieval preaching, both law and the gospel must be preached. Luther lamented that, "for many centuries there has been a remarkable silence about this (law and gospel) in all the schools and churches."[22] This prolonged silence contributed to an inadequate understanding of the doctrine of justification. It is the mark of a "real theologian" to know well how to distinguish radically between them. Both are of the same Word of God.[23] The "Pope has not only confused the law with gospel, but he changed the gospel into mere laws."[24] When the law is presented as the gospel, the law itself is lost. A real preacher must diligently know and maintain the distinction between law and gospel, without reducing the latter into the former, nor rejecting the former completely in favor of the latter. The ministry of the Word must proclaim both law and gospel. This is God's will and commission, and this is precisely what Christ himself has done. Henceforth Luther repudiated both legalism and antinomianism, "Both groups sin against the law: those on the right, who want to be justified through the law, and those on the left, who want to be altogether free of the law. Therefore we must travel the royal road, so that we neither reject the law altogether or attribute more to it than we should."[25]

The legalists, by their attempts to satisfy the law and to be liberated from it, have put themselves all the more under its yoke. "That is a crab's way of making progress, like washing dirt with dirt!"[26] This explains why the preaching of the law must be followed by the preaching of the gospel.

> We are not to preach only one of these words of God, but both . . . We must bring forth the voice of the law that men may be made to fear and come to a knowledge of their sins and so to repentance and a better life. But we must not stop with that, for that would only amount to wounding and not building up, smiting and not healing, killing and not making alive, leading down

22. *LW* 26, 115.
23. Ibid.
24. *LW* 26, 343.
25. Ibid.
26. *LW* 27, 13.

into hell and not bringing back again, humbling and not exalting. Therefore we must also preach the word of grace and the
promise of forgiveness by which faith is taught and aroused . . .
Accordingly man is consoled and exalted by faith in the divine
promise after he has been humbled and led to a knowledge of
himself by the threats and the fear of the divine law.[27]

The preaching of the law by itself, without the preaching of the gospel, works in us total despair, which in turn might lead us to the new sin of
hating God. However, this despair can be healed when we hear the word
of the gospel. The law is not God's final word. The negative aspects of
the law—it's terrors, judgments, and death—are not the goal but only the
means in God's hands. The law, under the consolation of the gospel, becomes a "disciplinarian that drives a man to Christ." This "is a comforting
word and a true, genuine, and immeasurably joyful purpose of the law."[28]
Being assured of this, Luther said, "I feel great comfort and consolation,
when I hear that the law is a disciplinarian to lead me to Christ rather than
a devil or a robber that trains me not in discipline but in despair."[29] The
law by itself works damnation, but with the gospel it works salvation.

The antinomians, on the other hand, taught that, since the law
contributes nothing to justification, the preaching of it is superfluous. It
suffices to preach the gospel, which by itself can work repentance and
forgiveness of sins. Although Luther agreed with them that the law is not
a way of salvation, he affirmed the disciplinary purpose of the law. To
abolish the law, as the antinomians did, is to abolish sin itself. "But if sin is
abolished, then Christ has also been done away with for there would no
longer be any need for him."[30] Not until we place ourselves under the law,
or under its terror, are we able to recognize the greatness of what Christ
does for us. The law was given with a view to justification. It is necessary
that the law be preached so that it might convict the sinner and drive
him to Christ. The law makes him despair of himself and his own ability
so that he expects nothing from himself but everything from Christ. The
knowledge of sin, which came through the law, is "a great blessing," that

---

27. *LW* 31, 364.

28. See *WA* 39, I, 446 as cited in Paul Althaus, *The Theology of Martin Luther*, 259–60.
Translated by Robert C. Schultz. Philadelphia: Fortress, 1972.

29. Ibid.

30. See *WA* 39, I, 546 as cited in Althaus, *The Theology of Martin Luther*, 258.

the sinner might seek healing in the gospel.[31] Since the law is God's own word, it must be preached and heard. To do otherwise, as the antinomians did, is to refuse to hear the truth of God.

Did Christ put an end to the law as the antinomians thought? Luther answers with a resounding no because they fail to see the importance of the law. He said, "Literally: the law lasted until Christ . . . At that time Christ was baptized and began to preach, when in a literal way the law . . . came to an end."[32] There is a time for each to fulfill its own proper function. Spiritually, the law does not rule the conscience after it has done its job in adequately disclosing the wrath of God and creating terror. Here one must say, "Stop, law!"[33] Now the gospel takes over, puts an end to the accusing voice of the law, and fills our hearts with joy and victory. When faith comes, the "theological prison of the law" comes to an end. "Therefore you are being afflicted by this prison, not to do you harm but to re-create you through the Blessed Offspring. You are being killed by the law in order to be made alive through Christ."[34] This does not mean the gospel puts an end to the voice of the law; rather it puts an end to the *negative* voice of the law. Insofar as Christ is raised in us, the law is quieted and emptied of its accusing power. The role of the law as "our custodian" comes to an end with the coming of Christ.[35] The theological use of the law continues to function in the life of the Christian, but as a "schoolmaster."[36] The Christian is never beyond law and gospel, which are "radically distinct from each other and mutually contradictory but very closely joined in experience."[37]

Preaching Christ as Sacrament and Example

Christ is the content of preaching. So, should we preach Christ as Savior only or as example only? For Luther, it is not an either/or, but a both/and, because Scripture presents Christ in two ways, first as gift and then as example. Christ's sacrificial death includes both the sacrament, which signifies the death of sin in us and is given to faith, and the example, which

31. See *WA* 39, I, 517 as cited in Ibid., 260.
32. *LW* 26, 317.
33. Ibid.
34. *LW* 26, 339.
35. *LW* 26, 345.
36. Ibid.
37. *LW* 26, 336.

behooves us to imitate him in bodily suffering and dying. Christ in the role of our righteousness and salvation is ontologically prior to the garment of imitation. The sequential order must be observed: Christ as gift must necessarily precede Christ as example.

The appropriate response to the sacrament of the crucified Christ is an "abstract faith," which has "putting on Christ and having all things in common with him" as its content.[38] This faith unites the soul with Christ like a bride with her bridegroom, making them into one person. Following his break with scholasticism and throughout the course of his career, Luther constantly upheld that abstract faith alone justifies. All that is required of the believer is to "cling in faith to this man, Christ, which is the sufficient and necessary condition," by which he receives in pure passivity Christ's "alien" righteousness.[39]

Luther then introduced the concept of an "incarnate faith," which is understood with works. Just as the body is followed by its shadow, so faith is to be followed by works. It is impossible to separate works from faith just as it is impossible to separate heat from fire. While it is true that faith alone justifies, without works, there cannot be a "genuine faith, which, after it has justified, will not go to sleep but is active through love."[40] Real faith must be active, seeking its concretization and validation in good works. The fruits bear testimony to the tree that produces them.

The theological impetus to act is understood as the inherent consequence of Luther's idea of incarnate faith. This idea helped Luther meet Karlstadt's and the Anabaptists' accusations that he had divorced faith from works. While at times Luther speaks of abstract faith, or naked faith without works, at other times he goes so far as to speak of an antithetical relationship between faith and works. "Faith does not perform work, it believes in Christ;" "all that is kept is faith, which justifies and makes alive."[41] It is from this perspective that Luther repudiated the soteriology of the Anabaptists, that the believer "must suffer many things . . . and imitate the example of Christ," arguing instead that faith "learns about Christ and grasps him without having to bear the cross."[42] He charged them for

38. *LW* 26, 264.
39. *LW* 26, 55.
40. *LW* 27, 30.
41. *LW* 26, 274.
42. *LW* 26, 270.

failing to distinguish between preaching Christ as gift and preaching him as example. Both forms of proclamation have their own time. If this is not observed, the proclamation of salvation becomes a curse. Here his pastoral advice on the proper time in which preaching is done is relevant,

> To those who are afraid and have already been terrified by the burden of their sins, Christ the savior and the gift should be announced, not Christ the example and the lawgiver. But to those who are smug and stubborn, the example of Christ should be set forth, lest they use the gospel as a pretext for the freedom of the flesh, and thus become smug.[43]

The function of the imitation of Christ corresponds to the function of the law as an alien work, leading us into inner conflict, death, and hell—not that we should perish, but that we might cleave to the prior and proper work of Christ's salvation. Good works performed in imitation of Christ will inevitably end in despair and failure. Christ as example is placed before our eyes so that we know we cannot equal it, "our light is like a burning straw against the sun." Our failure and despair remind us that we are still a saint and a sinner at the same time; they reveal "how much we are still lacking" in our faith. This lack can only be healed by embracing Christ again, but now as our savior, God's gift. This explains this writing of Luther,

> But I will not let this Christ be presented to me as exemplar except at a time of rejoicing, when I am out of reach of temptations (when I can hardly attain a thousandth part of his example), so that I may have a mirror in which to contemplate how much I am still lacking, lest I become smug. But in the time of tribulation I will not listen to or accept Christ except as a gift.

Preaching and the Holy Spirit

How does the preached Word become a personal word? How does one become convinced of God's redemptive act on the cross? Luther explained, "No one can correctly understand God or his Word unless he has received such understanding immediately from the Holy Spirit . . . outside of which nothing is learned but empty words and prattle."[44] The Holy Spirit's work

43. *LW* 27, 34.
44. *LW* 21, 299.

is not to reveal God apart from the incarnate Word. It is not his office to fill our hearts with glory separate from the cross. The Spirit creates faith in Christ. Faith, a gift of the Spirit, is justifying faith—faith in the incarnate and crucified Christ, which believes against reason and all appearances. Luther's understanding of the Spirit emerges in clear fashion in his response to the charismatic challenges to his doctrine of salvation. The central question addressed by Luther in his inquiry about Karlstadt is, "What makes a person a Christian?" To Luther, we are related to God through Jesus Christ, and are to trust him alone for salvation, not in the inner or mystical life, nor in outward behavior. So, says Luther,

> My brother, cling firmly to the order of God. According to it the putting to death of the old man, wherein we are following the example of Christ, as Peter says (1 Peter 2:21), does not come first, as this devil (Karlstadt) urges but comes last. No one can mortify the flesh, bear the cross, and follow the example of Christ before he is a Christian and has Christ through faith in his heart as an eternal creature. You can't put the old nature to death, as these prophets do, through works, but through the hearing of the gospel. Before all other works and acts you hear the Word of God, through which the Spirit convinces the world of its sin (John 8). When we acknowledge our sin, we hear the grace of Christ. In this Word the Spirit comes and gives faith where and to whom he wills. Then you proceed to the mortification and the cross and the works of love. Whoever wants to propose to you another order, you can be sure, is of the devil. Such is the spirit of this Karlstadt.[45]

The work of the Holy Spirit is to create faith by hearing the Word, which comes from outside of us in proclamation. Luther's quarrel with Karlstadt, Müntzer, and others is that they invert this order. "Dr. Karlstadt and these spirits replace the highest with the lowest, the best with the least, the first with the last. Yet he would be considered the greatest spirit of all, he who has devoured the Holy Spirit feathers and all."[46]

The Word and the Spirit are closely related like the voice and breath in speaking, "One cannot separate the voice from the breath. Whoever refuses to hear the voice gets nothing out of the breath either." God, who comes by the way of the cross, deals with us in a two-fold manner: first "outwardly," then "inwardly."

45. Ibid.
46. *LW* 40, 83.

Outwardly he deals with us through the oral word of the gospel and through material signs, that is baptism and the sacrament of the altar. Inwardly he deals with us through the Holy Spirit, faith, and other gifts. Whatever their measure or order, the outward factors should and must proceed. The inward experience follows and is effected by the outward. God has determined to give no one the Spirit or faith except through the outward. For he wants to give no one the Spirit or faith outside of the outward Word and sign instituted by him, as he says in Luke 16:29, 'Let them hear Moses and the prophets.' Accordingly Paul calls baptism a 'washing of regeneration' wherein God 'richly pours out the Holy Spirit' (Titus 3:5). The oral gospel is 'the power of God for salvation to everyone who has faith' (Rom 1:16).[47]

The order of salvation in Luther's theology begins with the Word addressing us, outside of us, through preaching what Christ has done for us, followed by the Word being heard and believed, and thereby we are saved by calling upon God. This order reflects the "whole root and origin of salvation," which "lies in God who sends."[48]

The work of the Holy Spirit is thus to communicate the gospel to us, which in Christ's cross and resurrection the divine blessing has conquered the divine curse. "The work [redemption] is finished and completed; Christ has acquired and won the treasure for us by his sufferings, death, and resurrection, etc."[49] But Christ's work remains of no avail if the Holy Spirit does not apply to us this treasure of salvation. "God has caused the Word to be published and proclaimed, in which he has given the Holy Spirit to offer and apply to us this treasure of salvation."[50] Therefore to sanctify is nothing else than to bring us to Christ to receive God's manifold blessings. By the Holy Spirit, we are led to Christ in whom the fatherly heart is found. The triune God works together as one in the economy of salvation. More fully,

Although the whole world has sought painstakingly to learn what God is and what he thinks and does, yet it has never succeeded in the least. But here you have everything in richest measure. In these three articles God has revealed and opened to us the most

47. *LW* 40, 146.

48. *LW* 25, 410.

49. See Luther's "Large Catechism," in *The Book of Concord*, 415. Edited by Theodore Tappert. Philadelphia: Fortress, 1959.

50. Ibid.

profound depths of his fatherly heart, his sheer, unutterable love. He created us for this very purpose, to redeem and sanctify us. Moreover . . . we could never come to recognize the Father's favor and grace were it not for the Lord Christ, who is the mirror of the Father's heart. Apart from him we know nothing but an angry and terrible judge. But neither could we know anything of Christ, had it not been revealed by the Holy Spirit.[51]

The Spirit confers in our hearts the assurance that God wills to be our Father, to forgive our sin, and to bequeath eternal life on us. The Spirit comes to inculcate the sufferings of Christ for our benefit. Only God can put the preached word in our hearts. Should God remain silent, the final effect is as though nothing has been spoken. The activity of the Holy Spirit is intrinsically bound to the Word that is spoken. Except the Holy Spirit draws, no one would come. When he draws, he does it not like a hangman, who drags a criminal up the ladder to the gallows, but as a kind man, who gently attracts by his amiability and cordiality so that people abide with him willingly and cheerfully.

Why do some repent earlier while others much later? Here Luther gives credence to the freedom of the Holy Spirit so that the control is taken out of the preacher's hand. The Holy Spirit works freely through the word in the manner appropriate to the specific context. In some cases, the word, which has been preached many years ago, may remain in the heart without effect; then God's Spirit comes, and gives new power to the formerly preached word, making it finally effective. The "whomever" and the "whenever" is the Spirit's prerogative, about which we can do nothing except to submit to his work. God wills that we should teach the law and shall see who will be converted by it. Just as the gospel is for all, and yet not all believe, so the law is for all, even though not everyone feels the power and significance of it. Why does preaching not meet always with the same level of effectiveness? This is hidden from us, and thus is not open to speculation. Our task is to remain faithful to preaching and hearing. Contrary to the enthusiasts, God's word enters our heart without any preparation or help on our part. There is only one true preparation and that is to hear or read or preach the word.

51. Ibid., 419.

Conclusion

The uniqueness of Luther's theology of preaching lies in that preaching is not mere human speech about God; rather it is God's own speech to human beings. Preaching is indeed the minister's activity; but it is also God's activity. When we hear a sermon, we do not hear the pastor. The voice is his, but the words he uses are really spoken by God. God meets us through the agency of human voice. Preaching is God's Word speaking to us, not a rehashing of old stories about him. Such an understanding casts light on the character of God, which is not the far-off deistic God, who is remote from the preached word and is only spoken about as if he were someone absent. The biblical God is not the impassive deity of the Greeks, but an ever-present deity who hides in human speech and is active in preaching through the human voice. Accordingly, the faithful hearers will respond, "Pay attention, we are hearing God's speech."[52]

Preaching Christ is not a discursive act, as is done in the university; rather it is the actual bestowal of Christ's benefits on the hearer. It nourishes the soul, makes it righteous, liberates it, and saves it. The Word is the power of Christ functioning in the act of preaching, through the preacher's mouth, to effect what has been proclaimed. Preachers assume the "right to speak," though not the "power to accomplish."[53] The efficacy of preaching lies not in human power or techniques, but rather in God's power. It is God's good pleasure to shine his Word in the heart through both law and gospel, but not without the external, spoken Word. What an office, a name, and an honor of preachers, to be "God's co-workers" to achieve his purpose![54]

52. *LW* 51, 288.

53. *LW* 51, 76.

54. See WA 17, 8, 179 as cited in Althaus, *The Theology of Martin Luther*, 40.

6

Enthusiasm Alone—Is It Enough?
(Romans 12:9–11; 1 Corinthians 13:1–8)[*]

Ralph Waldo Emerson wrote very accurately about enthusiasm,

> Enthusiasm is one of the most powerful engines of success. When
> you do a thing, do it with all your might. Put your whole soul into
> it; stamp it with your own personality. Be active, be energetic and
> be faithful, and you'll accomplish your object.

To be sure, none of us would have any difficulty with Emerson's words.
Even St. Paul would embrace them unhesitatingly, as he said in Romans
12:11, "Serve the Lord fervently." We are to serve with enthusiasm, with all
our might, soul, and the totality of our being, "Never be lacking in zeal,
but keep your spiritual fervor, serving the Lord."

Enthusiasm—everyone wants it. We thank God for the many enthusiastic ones in our church. Tyndale University College and Seminary (an
international institution strategically placed in the city of Toronto for the
training of Christians to serve the world with passion for Jesus Christ) is
no exception.

In this Graduation Chapel, on such a solemn but homely occasion, may I pose this question for our reflection together—is enthusiasm
enough to make a church grow? Is it enough to depend on enthusiasm
alone in order to grow a ministry, whatever that may be? The answer to
this question is an emphatic "no." St. Paul, a very zealous leader, did not
think that enthusiasm alone sufficed. It is good in itself, but by itself it can
never be good enough. It needs to be supplemented by other elements.

* With minor variations, this sermon was delivered at Graduation Chapel 2004 of
Tyndale University College & Seminary, Toronto, Ontario, Canada. Part of the materials
was shared in the Award Dinner, in which I was awarded the Tyndale Seminary Faculty
Excellence in Scholarship 2004.

In Romans 12:9–11, he mentions three elements to be combined with enthusiasm in the religious life of all ministers and Christian workers: enthusiasm, humility, and dedication to goodness.

Enthusiasm and Love

First, enthusiasm in service must be supplemented with true love, or affection. In the same text, Paul combines fervent service with passionate love. "Love must be sincere; be devoted to one another in brotherly affection" (vv. 9–10). Love is the greatest thing in the world, and the greatest need of humanity. We all need it, and some of us want it desperately. Young people cannot wait to fall in love. All of us become better and stronger precisely because of the loving affection we receive from others. But the more enthusiastic we are in our ministry, the more we need to be devoted to one another in the proximity of a loving affection. O, how I covet it—the combination of enthusiastic service and warm affection, the first pair of coincidental opposites.

In 1996, I was on a preaching trip to Eastern Europe. On the plane, I was reading about Florence Allshorn, one of the most distinguished Anglican women of the century. She founded the St. Julian Community and had a far-reaching influence in the world. As a young, fresh university graduate, Florence was commissioned as a missionary to Uganda. While there, she found a serious problem many missionaries have found, that it is much harder to get along with one's colleagues than to convert the unconverted.

In her mission station, the senior colleague had broken the nerves of seven of Florence's predecessors. Not one stayed there for more than two years. There was little doubt that she was a devout and brilliant leader. But her unpredictable moods and furious outbursts of temper were almost impossible to live with.

Florence served under her leadership for a year, and then her nerve began to go. One day, she was found crying her eyes out. An old African maiden came and said the most piercing thing that could ever be said to a missionary, "I have been here in this mission station for over fifteen years. Missionaries, educated and devoted, came out here, telling us that they have brought us a savior who could save to the utmost. But I have not seen this situation with all its problems and complexities saved yet."

What an anti-climax to hear something like that! In spite of this, Florence was determined to stay to make a difference. For one whole year, she read 1 Corinthians 13 to herself every day, Paul's marvelous hymn of praise to love. Then slowly things began to change. Finally, the glorious moment came when that senior colleague knelt down with Florence, confessed, and they were reconciled. She said to Florence: "I thank God for the day when the Lord called you here."

Deeply inspired by Florence's dedication, I too read 1 Corinthians 13 almost everyday. Since then, the text has become canonical in my daily meditation, and the teleological principle of all my works: scholarship, mentorship, teaching, and service. What great profits I have gained from such discipline, the excellent way of love as the *telos* of everything we do, be it at home, in church, or in any organizations to which we are committed.

Let me personalize 1 Corinthians 13:

> If I possess a dynamic faith that moves mountains, a thriving faith that can dream dreams, and turn them into action quickly, a filling faith that can drive a project and get it done efficiently, yet have no love, I am nothing.
>
> If my enthusiasm makes me a bully or drives people away, especially those who are slower, I am a clanging cymbal.
>
> If I send an unkind email towards those who are critical of my works in scholarship, I am nothing.
>
> If I become so task-oriented that I ignore the feelings of other people, I am nothing.
>
> If I show a lack of understanding and sympathy towards those who are weaker, I am nothing.
>
> If I confuse the slower with the weaker (the slower may not be the weaker), and see them as blockheads or blockages to the ministry, then I do not love.
>
> If I become irritable towards my son who just wants to be with me for a while in my study room, I am nothing.
>
> If I become envious of others who possess more accomplishments than me, and begin to eye them with suspicion, I do not love.
>
> If my enthusiasm runs down people, causing them misery, I am nothing.

If I become ill-mannered towards those who are my equals (spouse and colleagues), those who are under my care (my students), and those who are over me (presidents or the academic dean), then I am nothing.

If I give up myself and all my possessions for the needy, but do it not out of love as the prime motivation, then I am nothing, even though I am regarded by the public as the model of sacrifice.

Love understands; it seeks to walk alongside others; it appreciates the efforts of others; it is slow to attack, but quick to affirm. Love has good manners, it is not envious, it is not arrogant, and it does not use people as a platform for one's own virtue. Love trusts, hopes, and bears all; it never fails, and it endures forever.

Because of the pre-eminence of love, St. John of the Cross advised us solemnly: "When the evening of life comes, we will be judged on love."[1]

Enthusiasm and Dedication to Goodness

Second, Paul mentions another pair of elements: enthusiasm in service, and a dedication to do good and to shun evil. This is borne out in verse 9, "cling to what is good; shun what is evil," and in verse 11, "be fervent in your service." The challenge before us is to maintain the balance between fervency and sanity, devotion and decency. The temptation is to become so enthusiastic in our ministry that we become enthusiastically wicked or even insane, without knowing until it is brought to light. In the process of service, our dedication may undergo a major shift. Instead of seeking to do good, we give in to evil motives and hidden sins. We become twisted in our dedications, nurturing a lust of fame in our hearts. Driven by a certain pride in the power or authority entrusted to us by the organization, we live a life confounding and blurring the distinction between right and wrong, good and evil. May God preserve us from such dangers!

As much as we extol in the triumphant grace, there is still a dark side of human nature. We all suffer from the curvature of the human soul. Evil is like a boomerang; you fling it out and it will swerve back at you. The tendency is to maim and kill, to fight back when we are treated unjustly.

A story is told of an old woman in Dallas, Texas. She was driving a big limousine. Just when she was about to park, a young chap driving a little sports car nipped in and took the parking spot. Then he came to the

1. Quoted in John N. Gladstone, *A Magnificent Faith*, 63. Hantsport: Lancelot, 1979.

old woman and said, "Madam, that's what you can do when you are young and quick."

She was furious at him. So she backed up her limousine, and drove it against that little car, and squashed it into messy pieces. Then, laughing, she said to the young man: "Young man, that's what you can do when you are old and rich." That is the boomerang of evil, an eye for an eye.

But evil needs not triumph in our lives; it can be conquered by a dedication to do good. As a pastor and a public figure, for some reason I became an object of hate. An elder, in front of others in the office, pointed his finger at me: "You liar, why should we listen to you?" At that moment, I wished I was not a pastor but a "Kung Fu" fighter or a boxer. I was tempted to fill his mouth with my fist. However, I said to him kindly: "Brother, put your finger where it belongs. Your comment is an assault on my integrity, and integrity is all that we have. You should never say such a thing like that. I am too angry to talk with you. Don't come near me, for I may sin boldly and badly. You will hear from me in three months time." Later, we did meet, and the end result was repentance and reconciliation.

May I stress this, evil is not the final word, but God's grace is. Evil was dissipated; goodness has triumphed. Although the power of sin is still operative, it can be conquered by constantly availing ourselves of the sacramental causality of God's Word. God has promised to meet us in the Word and sacraments, the means by which he works transformation and sanctification in our lives. With a dedication to do good, evil can become a diminishing power. Russians often quote their hero Alexander Solzhenitsyn, who spoke eloquently about the stance that a good man must take,

> He will not participate in the lies.
> He will not share in the wickedness.
> Let evil come into this world,
> Let it even reign supreme, but only not through me.

As a daily exercise, we must ask: what good things can we do today for our family, church, or our workplace? We can do good to others by avoiding two major evils: gossip and blame. As regards the first evil, Charles H. Spurgeon advised us, "When you hear an evil report about anyone, halve it and quarter it, and then say nothing about the rest."[2] There are a lot of things that should not be passed around, even when they may be true. The purpose of fellowship and cell groups is to foster mutual care and proper

2. Quoted in Zuck, *The Speaker's Quote Book*, 176.

nurture in God's word. Avoid gossip of every kind, for it might destroy our mutual trust and weaken a good friendship.

We must also prevent the evil of blame from surfacing in leadership meetings. Whenever I sense that people are negative and they start finger pointing at each other, I close the meeting and turn it into a prayer meeting. One of the greatest poisons in a relationship is to blame others. Concerning the futility of blame, my mentor Charles Swindoll says,

> Blame never affirms; it assaults.
> Blame never restores; it hurts.
> Blame never solves; it complicates.
> Blame never unites; it separates.
> Blame never smiles; it frowns.
> Blame never forgives; it rejects.
> Blame never forgets; it remembers.
> Blame never builds; it destroys.

And it will destroy our fellowship and unity, if we resort to the practice of blame.

Enthusiasm and Humility

Finally, enthusiasm alone does not suffice; it must be completed by "honoring one another above ourselves (v. 10)." Humility means being the first to concede honor, taking the initiative to esteem others highly. Chrysostom expanded on this, "Humility is the mother, root, nurse, foundation and center of all other virtues."[3] Here is the third pair of elements: enthusiastic ministry and intentional humility.

Having been at Tyndale for nearly ten years, I have heard many great reports about our graduates. They earn respect from others and have made us proud. Unfortunately, from time to time, I have heard bad news about some of our graduates. It has been said that, during the first year of ministry at church, a pastor is idolized; in the second year, he is criticized; in his third year, he is ostracized; and after his fourth year, he is fired. For those who were fired, I am told this was done not because of ignorance but arrogance, setting themselves over others. An elder explained to me about the fate of one of my students who was fired: he is prideful, contentious, competitive, and always tries to outsmart others. He is more interested in proving what a scholar he is than in expressing love; more concerned

3. Zuck, *The Speaker's Quote Book*, 201.

about parading his learning than giving honor to others. He cannot work with people and his ego is bigger than his IQ.

Then he asked, "Professor Ngien, please don't send me another student who is a *Master* of Divinity but one who wishes to be the *Servant* of Divinity."

For those who are degree-intoxicated, I have some advice. After one week being the pastor in a church, nobody cares what academic degrees you have. They only care whether a real servant of God is there, to feed and care for their souls.

There is a chilling passage in a novel entitled *The Cathedral*. A clergyman, Father Brandon, is a very pompous and egotistical man. One day, one of the unruly members of his congregation, emboldened by drink, confronted him in the cathedral. Face to face with Father Brandon, he said,

> I have been waiting for this moment for years. Sunday after Sunday, week after week, I have seen you strutting about in this lovely place, the Cathedral, parading with pomposity, glorying in your power, and happy in your conceit. Your arrogance has been an insult to the very God you pretend to serve. I don't know whether there is a God. But there is this sacred, lovely Cathedral, fully alive, wonderful, majestic and serene, and you dare to set yourself above it, and all that it represents.

What a piercing statement! And Paul would have looked at Father Brandon, and said, "Away with your pomposity, parading, strutting, vanity, and haughtiness. You are not in the ministry for your own sake, but for the glory of God, the Most High, who calls you and without whom you are nothing, even though you think you are something."

Think about Tyndale and what it stands for. This institution contains many antecedents: the past labors, the legacies, numerous contributions, and many sacrifices that have preceded us. It is arrogance to set ourselves above them. Conversely, it is humility to acknowledge our reliance on what has come before us. We are the subsequent, and thus in many ways are the consequents. Thus we should never think we could create our own future *ex nihilo*, without any reference to the pre-existent materials that constitute Tyndale.

A Final Word to the Graduating Class

Beloved students, do remember the professors, staff, and those who have given of themselves for your benefit, and esteem them highly. Remember the antecedents of the church to which you are called, and honor them in a spirit of Christ-like humility. Be fervent in your service or whatever vocation God calls you to, while at the same time being the first to give honor, for that is part of what it means to be a servant of an illustrious Master.

Knowledge is power; scholarship is power; awards and degrees are power. But all of these could become a loveless power. They can turn what is supposedly a beautiful virtue into a deadly vice. Applying 1 Corinthian 13 again to us,

> If I have a gift of scholarship and have no love, I am nothing.
>
> If I possess the brainpower to think critically and preach eloquently, but have become puffed up, rude, and insensitive, then I am nothing.
>
> If I deem myself part of an intellectual elite, pontificating from the height of my intellectual capacity, and looking down contemptuously upon those who are of different breeds, then I am a resounding gong.
>
> If I, by the degrees I earn and the awards I receive, become an intellectual snob, then I am nothing.
>
> If I am entrusted with a position or power to lead, but take a dim view of those who don't measure up, I am a clanging cymbal.
>
> If one day I should have a quarrel with the church, let it be a lover's quarrel with it, the imperfect church for whom Christ dies.

So let us, as a community of faith, dedicate our lives to the proposition and power of love in a world largely given over to the fantasies and futility of power. Let the excellent way of love shine through our lives and our vocation, for this is the way of Christ. Let us take the beauty from Tyndale, and let it multiply out there. And let us go out from this noble place, to which we are indebted, and do something beautiful for Christ.

Glory to God in the Highest!

7

Picturing Christ: Martin Luther's Advice
on Preparing to Die*

I REMEMBER AN AFRICAN brother who stood in an evangelistic meeting and told how he was brought to Christ by his dying seven-year-old daughter. One day he heard her praying for his salvation, though she lay in bed debilitated by tuberculosis and malaria.

"Dad, do you believe in God?" she asked as he sat beside her.

"Oh, yes, darling; only a fool would deny God's existence."

"If you believe in God, you should also believe in eternal life."

"Oh, yes; if there is a God, there must be eternal life."

"But, dad, you don't have eternal life, for Jesus is not in your heart."

He reported, "Then my little daughter begged me to kneel beside her deathbed. I recited her words as she prayed for my conversion. 'O God, let Christ come into my heart. Please save my soul; give me eternal life.'"

Not all Christians face death so courageously. In the past twenty years, I have conducted and preached at more than 150 memorial and funeral services. I have sat beside numerous deathbeds, with people terrified by the sight of the final conflict. For me, it is no wonder that Scripture calls death "the last enemy."

This brother, now advanced in years, is battling cancer and is face to face with his own death. Knowing how fierce this last battle can be, I sent him one of the most helpful meditation guides I've known, Martin Luther's *A Sermon on Preparing to Die*. In this sermon, Luther provides pastoral counsel to his closest friend, Mark Schart, who was troubled by thoughts of death. His counsel contains a great deal of wisdom for today.

---

* This article was published in *Christianity Today* (April, 2007): 66–69.

6

The Three Temptations

Luther believed that death becomes ominous because the devil uses it to undermine our faith. He haunts us with death in three ways.

First, the Devil taunts us with the remembrance that death is a sign of God's wrath toward sinners. "In that way, [the devil] fills our foolish human nature with the dread of death while cultivating a love and concern for life, so that burdened with such thoughts man forgets God, flees and abhors death, and thus, in the end, is and remains disobedient to God."

Luther's remedy for this first temptation is to contemplate death all the more, but to do so at the right time—which is not the time of death. Instead, he exhorts us to "invite death into our presence when it is still at a distance and not on the move"—that is, in our daily lives long before death threatens us. Conversely, Luther counsels Christians to banish thoughts of death at the final hour and to use that time to meditate on life.

Second, the Devil magnifies our accusing conscience by reminding us of those who were condemned to hell for lesser sins than ours. This, too, casts us into despair, so that we forget God's grace in the last hour. Again Luther admonishes us not to deny our sinfulness, but to contemplate it during our lifetimes, as is taught in Psalm 51:3, "My sin is ever before me." The devil closes our eyes to our sin during our lives, just when we should be thinking of it. He then opens our eyes to the horrible reality of sin and judgment in the final hour, when our eyes should be seeing only grace.

Third, the Devil plagues us with the prospect of hell, specifically by increasing the soul's burden with haunting questions concerning election. He prods the soul into undertaking the one thing forbidden—delving into the mystery of God's will. In this undertaking, the devil "practices his ultimate, greatest, and most cunning art and power," for he "sets man above God" so that we look in the wrong place for assurance of election. In this respect, delving into the mystery of election is never a good practice, but especially not when one faces the final enemy.

Christ: Sheer Life

How do we banish these devilish images and see only grace? Luther exhorts us to contemplate the image that saves: Jesus Christ, who "overcame death with life." In addition, he encourages us to contemplate the deaths of those who died in God's grace, such as the saints before us. The more one fixes one's gaze on such pictures, the more death appears "contemptible and dead, slain and overcome in life. For Christ is nothing other than sheer life, as his saints are likewise."

Luther says to look to Christ is to see grace, because "the picture of grace is nothing else but that of Christ on the cross."

> Here sins are never sins, for here they are overcome and swallowed up in Christ. He takes your death upon himself and strangles it so that it may not harm you, if you believe that he does it for you and see your death in him and not in yourself. Likewise, he also takes your sins upon himself and overcomes them with his righteousness out of sheer mercy, and if you believe that, your sins will never work you harm.

Luther also says that when facing death's agonies, we should find support in the fellowship and faith of the church. The experience of dying, though intensely personal, cannot be handled privately without our being crushed. As each person contends with death, we should not desert him or leave him to die alone. In the deafening loneliness of death, we "shout in the ears" of the dying to assure them of our companionship. In fact, God, Christ, angels, saints, and the entire congregation "shout" with us. The eyes of the entire communion of saints are upon the dying to empower him to go through the unavoidable. The annihilating voice of death, then, can drive us into the arms of Christ. The voice of the law that incites sin, death, and divine wrath is replaced by the voice of the gospel. That voice is like a lamp shining in darkness until the day dawns and the morning star rises in our hearts (see 2 Peter 1:19–20)—and it makes dying much easier.

Born Again

Death, for Luther, is "the beginning of the narrow gate and of the straight path to life" (Matt 7:14). Although the gate is narrow, the journey is not long. Luther elaborates,

> Just as an infant is born with peril and pain from the small abode of its mother's womb into this immense heaven and earth . . . so man departs this life through the narrow gate of death. . . . Therefore, the death of the dear saints is called a new birth, and their feast day is known in Latin as *natale*, that is, the day of their birth.

This road through the dark valley may be traveled safely when we are assured of its end. We do not have to deny the pain of grief and death. On the contrary, it is the harsh reality of death that makes the heavenly mansion so glorious, "So it is that in dying we must bear this anguish and know that a large mansion and joy will follow."

While we should be aware daily of the inevitable reality of death, we can live as those who have been freed from the curse and sting of death. Luther wisely reminds us to ponder "the heavenly picture of Christ," for in Christ, we have passed from death to life. Death is no death to the believers whose lives are hidden with Christ in God.

8

The Image of a Heart-broken Father
(Hosea 11:1–11)[*]

IN THE FIRST TEN chapters of Hosea, the emphasis is on divine judgment on Israel's sin. From chapter 11 onwards, there is a shift, with the focus moving from divine judgment to a wonderful display of the love of God. The dominant note of chapters 11–14 is that of God's conquering, unfailing, unfrustratable, and utterly irresistible love. The fundamental relationship between God and Israel is based on a covenant in which God swore: "Israel will be my people, I will be their God." God loves them sovereignly.

All love, if it is true love, is sovereign. If a man loves his wife because she is beautiful or able that is not sovereign love, but conditional and often selfish love. When God loves, he does not tell us why. He loves because he loves. The divine choice of Israel was an act of pure sovereign love, not based upon the nation's merit or importance, and independent of human performances or credit.

In the earlier chapters, the relationship between God and Israel was likened to that between a husband and his wife, the faithful Hosea and his harlot wife, Gomer. Here in chapter 11, God is pictured as a loving father, and Hosea writes of God's fatherly love in reference to Israel's past, present, and future. This chapter is one of the most powerful portrayals of the heart of God for the undeserving and unworthy.

---

* The sermon was delivered at *Knox Summer Fellowship 2007*, an annual ecumenical gathering held at *Knox Presbyterian Church*, Toronto, Ontario. Canada. Monumentally, this was the first sermon heard by my nine-year-old Hansel, who sat at *Trinity Mandarin Presbyterian Church*, Toronto, seeing his daddy in action. He commented: daddy's preaching was "too hyper," meaning passionate.

The Image of a Heart-broken Father

God's Paternal Grief over Israel (vv. 1–7)

In verses 1–4, God begins to speak as a heartbroken father. The love of the father is expressed through a series of tender images or figures. Notice that there is a historical recital in God's monologue, i.e., God is speaking in an "I" voice, recalling his electing love for Israel. Verse 1 reads, "When Israel was a child, I loved him, out of Egypt I called my son." And verse 3 says, "It was I who taught Ephraim to walk, taking them by the arm." Ephraim, being the largest of the ten tribes in the Old Testament Northern Kingdom, is often used as a synonym for Israel. I remember when my child first began to walk, I was behind him guiding him, with my hands on his little hands, and his little feet on my two big feet so that he got a sensation of what walking is like. That was precisely what God did to Israel. When cuts and bruises came, God says, "I was the one who healed them," like a nurse would do. When Israel developed into adulthood, God's love remained unwavering. Likening himself to a romantic lover, God says in verse 4, "I led them with cords of human kindness, with ties of love; I lifted the yoke from their neck, and bent down to feed them." Using imagery from the field, God is compared to the herdsman who drives the heifer, which toils for him. God says, "I will draw them by cords of rope, as a man does, but by the cords of love, not of slavery." There was no harsh driving, but only tender, gentle driving. He eased the strain and burden and compassionately led them. When evening came, the herdsman led them home, lifted the yoke from their neck, and liberated them for rest and eating. God says, this is what I have done for you, O Israel. In condescending love, I bent down and fed you.

God also says, "I am the father who loved you, called you out of Egyptian bondage, taught you by the laws I gave you, guiding you, supporting you, healing you, and feeding you so that you could be said, at the end of the day, to lack nothing." God has done all these things in relation to his covenant people. But how did they respond to the tender loving care of Jehovah? "They went from me," the Lord complains; "they sacrificed to the Baals and burnt incense to images" (v. 2). "They did not know that I healed them" (v. 3), meaning they did not acknowledge him at all. They refused to return to God, and were bent on declension or backsliding (v. 5). Verse 7 concludes, "My people are determined to turn from me." Paternal grief and sadness are evident towards the end of part one of this poem.

The contrast is strikingly sharp. On the one hand, we see Jehovah, the persistent lover; on the other hand, Israel, the persistent reprobate, utterly unresponsive and ungrateful. They lived in God's bounty, yet they did not return thanks to God. Instead of worshipping Jehovah, they gave their devotion to the Baals. The sin of God's people is heightened in light of what God has graciously done for them. In the light of the intensity of the love with which God loves them, their rebellion against God is all the more painful for him.

There is an irrational absurdity in Israel's change of religious affection. It is not as though they have been underprivileged, deprived, or in an abusive relationship, and have now found the father of their dreams in the Baals, and thus transferred their affection to a carved piece of wood. Not at all! Israel's rebellion is against the sweetest, tenderest, and most generous of loves. It is not as though they have found in the Baals a better deity, a greater revelation or love, a more wonderful provider, a greater light, or a greater reality or liberty. Not so! They have departed from the Supreme Good, in whom their being and well-being consist. They have departed from the Superlative Love. Though they paid lip service to the Most High, their hearts were fixed on departure from the Most High (v. 7), the very source of their being and the very sustenance of their well-being.

Israel's descent into sin incurred disastrous consequences (vv. 5–6). Divine judgment would be their portion. God punished them severely by causing the Assyrians to invade their land, destroy their cities, demolish all lines of defenses, and put an end to their plans. Verse 6 reads, "The swords would be upon them." Though they cried out to the Most High for help, help would not come. They must feel the wrath of God. The outcome is that Assyria would be their king and hold them in captivity.

Many translations and commentators change the opening clause of verse 5 into a question (will they not return to Egypt?), arguing that Israel will go back to Egypt. Hosea has been using Egypt as a metaphor for slavery or bondage. What is being said is not that Israel will return to Egypt literally, but the nation will return to bondage as symbolized by Egypt (v. 6). This time the judgment will take them to Assyria. The juxtaposition of Egypt and Assyria is of theological importance. Just as they had felt the force of divine judgment while in exile in Egypt, so now they would feel the terror of divine judgment under Assyrian domination. Just as God caused them to be in exile in Egypt, God now causes Assyria to invade them. And yet they would suffer a more severe outcome, for Assyria would treat them harshly as any king does to rebels.

The fate of a stubborn, rebellious son under the law was to be stoned to death (cf. Deut 21:18–21). Under Assyrian rule, Israel would be permanently exterminated, never again to be revived. But would God turn his back upon Israel, as it were to change the lock, phone number, or email so that all contacts with him are cut off? Would God return all the letters unopened? Would God give them up to utter destruction because they provoked his holiness and sinned against his faithfulness? Part 2 of the text answers these questions.

God's Passionate Love for Israel (vv. 8–9)

In this section, we see God's passionate love for the rebellious nation portrayed in a radical anthropomorphic language. In the form of divine monologue, a distinctive form of Hebrew poetry, God cries out for wayward Israel. With four escalating bitter cries, God questions himself in verse 8,

> How can I give you up, O Ephraim?
> How can I hand you over, O Israel?
> How can I treat you like Admah?
> How can I make you like Zeboim?

These correspond to the four declarative "nots" in verse 9:

> I'll not carry out my fierce anger;
> I'll not turn and destroy Ephraim.
> I am God, not man—the Holy One among you.
> I'll not come in wrath.

Sandwiched in between the four "hows" and four "nots" is God's own resolution, "My heart is changed within Me, and My compassion is aroused."

In this dialogue God has within himself, we perceive the dynamics of the opposing forces within God's own heart: law and grace, mercy and wrath are at war with each other. The divine heart is inwardly torn between punitive justice and the overflowing compassion of "not-letting-go" Israel. The conflicting emotions are most revelatory of the severity of God's struggle and pain within himself in the way he relates to his covenantal people. His heart becomes a battleground in which divine compassion and divine justice do battle with each other. And yet it is precisely in these contraries or antinomies wherein the beauty and depth of God's love are most manifested. Only God can endure these opposing forces or conflicting emotions without being crushed by them. As humans, we cannot endure such intense polarities without being handicapped by them. We cannot maintain a perfect balance between love and severity without going off-balance, or tending towards one extreme or the other—either towards over-permissiveness or over-harshness—and in the process we destroy others and ourselves.

But God is God, not man. Theology must observe the radical distinction between God and man, and not subject God to any creaturely passions. Being unique, God can endure the opposition in order to conquer it, and through this he creates a people no longer under his wrath. God can feel, yet without being held captive by those feelings. For our sake, God cuts through the knots of agonizing alternatives and finally creates hope out of despair.

The Lord knows that Israel deserves punishment. He has every right to execute his wrathful judgment upon them and destroy them as he did to Ahmah and Zeboim, the two smaller cities that shared the same fate as Sodom and Gomorrah. It is not as though the Lord does not know what he is doing, or what Israel's descent to sin might incur. Nescience (ignorance) is not one of his essential attributes. Hosea portrays God as inwardly divided, caught in a tension, conflict, or struggle with himself, vacillating between giving up Israel totally or sparing them mercifully. The deeper he loves, the greater is the tension he feels within himself. And the greater the tension, the greater the pain he feels because he wills to love the object of his wrath, the one who deserves something else.

What is it that holds him back from giving them up totally? It is nothing other than his immutable love, expressed in these words, "My heart turns within me, or turns against me. My compassion overflows; or it is stirred, being stirred to burn brighter. It is becoming hot. My compassion burns in my bosom passionately for the wayward sinner."

Justice comes with its claims; Israel's sins are great and many; they deserve God's wrath. However, mercy steps out and pleads,

> But, o Lord, art thou not their God? They have a multitude of sins. But is there no other way of dealing with the severity of their sins? Are they not the covenantal people? Have you not established a special relationship with them? Have you not pledged your love to them? So spare them, O Lord, for their fathers' sake.

When the Lord hears mercy pleading like that, he cries out four times, "How can I give them up?" And four times, he declares "I will not."

Judgment, as Isaiah 28:21 said, is God's strange work, an alien work, a work he does not at all enjoy performing. He was compelled into it by the wickedness of man. Divine wrath is not an essential attribute of God, but is a response called into being by the insults of sin. But he delights in mercy, for mercy is that which God is, not that which he possesses. This is why he repeatedly declares that his wrath is not the final word.

God said, "I am God, not man. I will not come in wrath." This verse is not to be taken to mean that God stops all judging. Judgment will come, but not as severely as it could. As heartbroken as he is, as inwardly torn as he is, he is not saying that he will withhold all judgment. What he does say is that he will not give them up as he did Sodom and Gomorrah. When judgment falls, it will not be in proportion to the severity of their sins. For sure, the Holy One in their midst remains holy and will get angry because of sin. Unlike human anger, God's anger is not a childish loss of temper. Nor is it a frustrated love turned sour or a wounded pride turned vindictive. For sure, he'll execute judgment, but not to the full extent of their sins. He does not judge like man, who often executes justice without restraint, but with vindictive anger. On the contrary, God said, "I'll not hand you over to Assyria, who will judge you harshly with an unmitigated justice, with the end result being dissolution or destruction. I will not come in wrath in the way Assyria did."

Judgment will come; wrath will be poured out; the calamity or ruin will be huge. But they will not be in proportion to what their rebellion calls for. Israel's ruin is bad enough, but it is nothing compared to what they really deserve, extinction. Even in their ruin, Israel could still sing of God's mercy. For, in God's wrathful judgment, he remembers his overflowing mercy; he remembers his people, his children, and his oath. God lives the love he pledges to Israel, a concrete proof of the reliability and constancy of God's character.

So what was it about God's people that could cause God to be lenient, to temper justice with mercy? Is divine leniency generated by some good qualities, which God has overlooked in the past but now discovers in Israel? Not at all! Nothing in Israel causes divine leniency; but there is something in God that causes him to move towards Israel with these passionate cries, "How can I possibly abandon it to extinction?" That something is "love"—that is who God is. The depth of God's being is love, eternally so. Luther said, "If I were to paint a picture of God, I would so draw him that there would be nothing else in the depth of his divine nature than that of fire and passion, which is called love for people."[1] The Godness of God, Luther further asserted, is "nothing but burning love and a glowing oven full of love."[2] And that is the abiding basis for Israel's being and well-being.

God's Promise to Israel (vv. 10–11)

Finally, in verses 10–11, God promises Israel their final restoration. Two things will happen following his fierce judgment. First, there will be a physical restoration (v. 11). Israel will not be completely wiped out; they will enjoy the blessing of the covenant. There will be a final homecoming. Those who have fled to Egypt for refuge will return hastily like birds out of Egypt; others will return swiftly like doves out of Assyria. They will dwell in their lands, and enjoy the freedom that has long been withheld.

Secondly, there will be a spiritual restoration. Verse 10 says, "They will walk after the Lord." The metaphor of a *lion*, used in Hosea 5 as a chastening wrath, reappears in this section. It speaks of God's majestic reign and power, which continues to pour out his chastening wrath. This is not done so that they might be consumed, but that they might turn to God for redemption. Thus God's wrath, symbolized by a roaring lion, has as its end the final restoration of Israel. As an alien work, God smites; as a proper work, he saves. The former leads to the latter. Hidden in the "no" is the "yes" of God. God judges so that Israel might come trembling and humble to the God of their covenant. Following the fierceness of God's wrath, at the signal of a roaring lion, the fear of the Lord might be planted in people's hearts and they might turn back to embrace the living God.

God's wrath is not just for punishing. God does not punish simply because they deserve to be punished. The chief purpose of God's chastening wrath is not that divine justice is glorified, but that people can be saved. God smites so that they can live with eternity in their hearts. God pours out his wrath not to destroy them finally, but so that they can be awakened from their spiritual slumber, or sensual insanity, which they

---

1. Quoted in Althaus, *The Theology of Martin Luther*, 116.
2. Ibid.

might see for themselves the horror of their sinfulness. Through his alien work (wrath), they come to realize that they cannot sneer at God and get away with it. God sent his wrath so that they can be brought to see that their sins have temporal consequences. Having seen this, they may come to realize their sins might also have eternal consequences. And having seen the eternal consequences of sin, they may repent and return to embrace the salvation of their Lord. At the end, there will be godliness and godlikeness, the fruits of God's alien work.

What is true love? True love, for Luther, is "wrathful love."[3] There is a wrath that belongs essentially to love. A father who does not get angry is hardly a loving father. A loving father does get angry with a wayward son. For him to be indifferent to whatever his rebellious son does is the opposite of love. The fact that he is wrathful shows he really cares. For the child that a father loves, he chastises or punishes. However, the ultimate end of fatherly wrath is remedial, not destruction.

Likewise, a God who does not get angry is hardly the God of the Bible. A God who could sit idly by and allow Israel's sin to work itself out to its logical conclusion (destruction) is not a loving God. Israel's God is not the unmoved deity or impassive deity of the Greeks, but is a passionate God who fights for the welfare of his people. He opposes anything that stands between himself and his people. He pours out a wrathful opposition against sin in order to conquer it. Thus we can speak of the anger of a loving God, for such anger emanates from a heart which is "nothing but burning love." The pouring out of his roaring wrath is an expression of his pure love. This wrathful opposition to sin is not generated by some abstract principle of justice, which demands retribution for the broken law; rather it is generated by a holy love, which demands a pure, undefiled relationship. He truly condemns, but only so that they can be placed within the orbit of his blessings. Therefore, divine wrath is not vindictive; it is the love of God burning hot in the presence of sin, proof that he does care. God elicits his wrathful opposition against all that stands between himself and his people in order to lead them back into the glowing oven full of his love.

Wrath is God's alien work of judging and humbling through which God performs his proper work of saving and exalting. So, at the sound of

---

3. Quoted in Philip Watson, *Let God Be God*, 159. Philadelphia: Muhlenberg, 1948.

God's wrathful roar, or rather wrathful love, Israel would be humbled by the divine majesty and return trembling to God.

God promises that there will be a final homecoming. His promise is no empty solicitude; it is efficacious and will be fulfilled. The details of how and when this will happen is hidden from us. But what is not hidden is that God's wrath is not the final word; instead, God's wondrous, invincible, efficacious grace is. His electing love is stronger than Israel's disobedience. Hence we break out into praise in the words of a hymn,

> The Love of God, so rich and pure,
> How measureless and strong;
> It shall forever endure,
> The saints' and angels' song.

Concluding Reflections: The Fruits

There are three specific fruits that can be gleaned from this piece of Hebrew poetry.

First, we must take our sin seriously, always be in touch with the gravity of our sinfulness, the depth of our wickedness, the curvature of the human soul. By nature, we are no better than Israel. Sin is sin; it remains horrible and destructive, if it is not judged. God is God, who is still the Holy One in our midst. His transcendence is not obliterated at the expense of his immanence. We should never assume that we can sneer at God and get away with it. God is God, and his holy love burns hot in the face of unrighteousness. At times he might come upon you with a wrathful roar in order to drive you home to his loving arms. Afflictions and crises are instruments of God's wrathful love, which God employs to place us within the orbit of his grace. He chastises us so that we might earnestly seek God, our only help and hope in our miseries. Hence, if God captures your attention by means of his alien work through a wrathful roar, then thank God for the fatherly chastisement, for whoever he loves, he disciplines.

Secondly, if we need to take sin seriously, then we ought to take his invincible grace far more seriously. To sin is to place ourselves under divine wrath, against which we cannot do anything except cleave to the God of mercy. Therefore, delight in his grace; run to him, the cleansing fountain, filled with his blood. For God is more willing to come to us than we are to come to him; he is more than willing to befriend us than we are to have a friend; he is more eager to forgive us than we are to repent.

Draw near to him for he has drawn very near to us in Jesus Christ. To put ourselves outside the realm of God is to deprive us of God's manifold blessings, eventually leading to self-dissolution. We can boldly approach God, as St. Anselm did in his *Proslogion*, asking God daily for more of his divine beauty,

> O God, I pray, let me know and love You, so that I may rejoice in You. And If I cannot in this life [know, love, and rejoice in You] fully, let me advance day by day until the point of fullness comes. Let knowledge of You progress in me here and be made full [in me] there. Let love for You grow in me here and be made full [in me] there, so that my joy may be great with expectancy while there being full in realization.[4]

Finally, no matter how far we have strayed, how deep our sins have been, in God's eyes, we are forever priceless. We are worth the precious blood of Jesus Christ. As Charles Wesley wrote, "And can it be that I should gain an interest in my Savor's blood."

A teacher held up a $20 bill and asked the class, "Who wants this $20 bill?" Every hand went up. The teacher said, "I am going to give this $20 bill to one of you." He took the bill and began to crumble it up, and then he asked, "Who still wants it?" All hands went up; they all wanted it. The teacher asked, "What if I do this?" He dropped the bill on the ground, and grinded it into the dirty floor. The bill is crumbled and dirty. Then he asked, "Now, who still wants this $20 bill?" Again, all hands were up.

"Now you learn an invaluable lesson. No matter what I do with the money, you still want it because it does not decrease its value. It remains $20, without any change in worth."

How many times have we been dropped by circumstances, tainted by dirt, or frustrated by wrong decisions made in a moment of fury? We may feel as though we are worthless. And yet no matter what happens, we'll never lose our value in God's eyes. This finds an echo in Luther who wrote, "Sinners are lovely because they are loved by God; they are not loved because they are lovely."[5] Dirty or crumbled, we are forever God's very own. St. Paul proclaimed: "Nothing, not even death, is able to separate us from the love of God that is in Christ Jesus."

4. *Anselm of Canterbury*, 112. Edited and translated by Jasper Hopkins and Herbert Richardson. London: SCM, 1974.

5. Luther, "Heidelberg Disputation," in *Martin Luther's Basic Theological Writings*, 48. Edited by Timothy Lull. Philadelphia: Fortress, 1989.

The matchless grace of God is stronger than all our sins. Although we may break his heart by our disobedience, his love is unbreakable. It continues to burn for us, saying, "I cannot give you up. I will not, I will not, I will not let you go." With a love like that, there is simply no reason that we should repudiate it. Let's welcome God's love to our hearts, and reciprocate his with our own.

> Love so amazing, so divine,
> demands my soul, my life and my all.

9

A Wise Rebuke—An Instrument of Divine Power
(Ecclesiastes 7:5–6)*

As THE FOUNDER OF the Centre for Mentorship and Theological Reflection, I am encouraged by the largest crowd we have had so far attending the Centre's annual event, which is often known as "Theology and Worship Night." Present here are scholars, educators, pastors, members of the laity, and students, most of whom have a busy life, but have chosen to come regularly to our annual event. Many have expressed to me that they have found this event inspiring, instructive, and nurturing. I am also impressed by the ecumenical character of our attendees, with various cultures, colors, languages, and races represented, all of which are the living embodiment of the incarnate Christ, our Lord and Savior.

Having heard Dr. Packer's weighty and enjoyable lecture, "Evangelicalism and the Future," Dr. Michael Haykin's ardent commendation of Packer's scholarship and his worldwide contributions, the Rev. Dr. John Kao's poignant response, and Dr. Rebecca Idestrom's salient remarks, each in their unique and distinct ways, what more can I add?

My wife, Ceceilia, kindly alerted me to the quality of these speakers. She issued me with a challenge, "Your final speech must not be an anti-climax for the occasion. Share something from your heart that might incite the people of God towards the path of righteousness." I shall hope to fulfill her expectation, and the final word is taken from Ecclesiastes 7:5–6,

> It is better to hear the rebuke of the wise
> than the song of the fools.

* This exhortation was delivered at The Centre for Mentorship and Theological Reflection's annual event held June 7, 2007, where notable scholars were honored: the Rev. Dr. J. I. Packer as the Senior Scholar, the Rev. Dr. John Kao as the Senior Churchman, and Dr. Rebecca Idestrom as the Research Scholar.

Like a crackling of thorns under the pot,
   so is the laughter of the fools.
This too is meaningless.

The Song of the Fool

What is the song of the fool? It is flattery—the insincere praise of others. Unfortunately, many of us develop a gluttonous appetite for such praise. We receive blatant flattery with open arms, without filtering it through our minds. In the process we become oblivious to the absurdity and insincerity of flattery, the song of the fools. No wonder we are off balance and our perspectives on things become distorted. Because we base our lives on lies, on the faint praises of others, we are weakened; we become shallow and superficial.

To be sure, genuine praise is good and must be shared. We all need it, and we are better and stronger precisely because of the genuine appreciation we receive from others. How I wish that we did this more in our church, friendships, and families! To withhold applause when it is rightly due is to commit a sin of omission.

But the applause of the fool must be repudiated because it is filled with lies. It must be dismissed as worthless, however soothing it is to hear. Alistair Begg, the Scottish preacher, said it well, "Flattery is like perfume; sniff it but don't swallow it. It will destroy you." Like the crackling of sticks burning under a pot (v. 6), generating much noise but completely unable to achieve its goal to do the task of cooking, the praise or flattery from a fool is worthless and meaningless. It is devoid of efficacy, totally unproductive, and has no instructional value. So to live life with superficial laughter is one mark of a fool. May God help us to see the futility, absurdity, and stupidity of the song of the fools!

The Reproof of the Wise

The preacher of the Ecclesiastes propounds a sharp contrast, "It is better to hear the rebuke of the wise." Notice the qualifying words, the rebuke of the *wise*, *not* of the *scoffers*, those who scorn you, who are spiteful and contemptuous. Make sure that it is a wise correction. The worth of a correction lies in the wisdom and spirit of the one who offers it. Censoriousness, carping, slander, sarcasm, and malice do not belong to the essence of true wisdom. These traits are not only unwise; they are also unchristian. They make the souls of the hearers sick, for their criticisms proceed from souls that are sick. To these sick souls, we say, "heal thyself before we hear your comments."

Great is the one who can accept criticism. Greater yet is the one who welcomes it. But greatest of all is the one who knows how to administer it in the spirit of love and sensitivity, without causing humiliation of the hearer. If our rebuke is not creatively given and wisely offered, people will resent it vindictively. But if correction is gently and sympathetically administered, it could be a vital stimulus for self-examination and personal edification. We should receive these suggestions, however painful they may be.

Historical Examples

People of influence have discovered the indelible value of a wise reproof. Instead of spurning it, they regard it as an instrument of divine power through which God efficaciously works his saving purpose. Not many could rise to the height of George Whitfield, the well-known British preacher of the eighteenth century. One time John Wesley found fault in him, and wrote a letter of rebuke to him. Whitfield's saintly reply was, "John, I thank you most heartily for your kind rebuke. I can only say it is too tender. I beseech you, whenever you see me do wrong, rebuke me sharply."[1] Here is a humble man who welcomes the rebuke that proceeds from a heart that is wise. No wonder God used him mightily. Although they differed theologically, George did not ignore John's advice. John's reproof had become the selected instrument God employed to work in him.

Calvin, one of the greatest reformation theologians, was trained in law and the classics. By nature, he shrank from the heat of controversy. In Geneva, when the reformation blossomed, he was instrumental at the beginning. Then he determined to return to France, to the peace and quiet of his library and profession. On the night before he left, a reformer named William Farel met him and rebuked him for holding back from offering help at such a needy time. In the preface to his *Commentary on the Psalms*, Calvin left his own record of this solemn reproof,

> William Farel forced me to stay in Geneva not so much by advice or urging as by command, which had the power of God's hand laid violently upon me from heaven. Since the wars had closed the

1. Cited in John Gladstone, *Living with Style*, 114. Burlington: Welch, 1986.

direct road to Strasbourg, I had meant to pass through Geneva quickly and had determined not to be delayed there more than one night. A short time before, by the work of the same good man and of Peter Viret, the papacy had been banished from the city; but things were still unsettled and the place was divided into evil and harmful factions. One man, who has since shamefully gone back to the papists, took immediate action to make me known. Then Farel, who was working with incredible zeal to promote the gospel, bent all his efforts to keep me in the city. And when he realized that I was determined to study in privacy in some obscure place, and saw that he gained nothing by entreaty, he descended to cursing, and said that God would surely curse my peace if I held back from giving help at a time of such great need. Terrified by his words, and conscious of my own timidity and cowardice, I gave up my journey and attempted to apply whatever gift I had in defense of my faith.[2]

So by a rebuke, an instrument of God's power, Calvin, weary of conflict and conscious of his own weaknesses, was brought to life and saved for the cause. He applied the gift he had in the service of the church. No one could deny his contribution and influence in Christianity.

Personal Examples

Over twenty-five years ago, at 2:00 a.m., my mother and I had a sacred conversation, one that was filled with motherly affection for the onerous son that I was.

I said, "Mom, what are you doing staying up? What is in your mind?"

She stuttered, "Baby boy, I don't know how to phrase it, to make it easier for you to hear what I am about to tell you. I have been worried sick about what I saw in you. I observed in you a certain lust for vainglory and vain conceit. I am fearful that they might eventually cause your downfall. Son, you either face them and conquer them, and as a result become a blessing to many, or you'll be strangled by a vain conceit you are nurturing in your heart."

That was a painful rebuke. For the first time, I was compelled to look deep within, and was horrified, as my mom was, by the magnitude of the evil within my heart. Most often God hides from us the full revelation of

2. See Commentary on Psalms, 53. Translated by Joseph Haroutunian. Library of Christian Classics, vol. 23. Philadelphia: Westminster, 1958.

the horror of our innermost evil. He keeps the magnitude of evil hidden so deeply that we become insensitive to it, or we do not feel it or think of it. But through a mother's harsh rebuke, God offered me a taste of the revelation of the evil within me. He then began his surgical work in me, breaking down all self-pretenses, self-confidence, and self-righteousness. To put it theologically, I felt the force of Luther's law-gospel distinction at work in me; it is God's alien work of humbling through the law in order to achieve his proper work of exalting in the gospel. The rebuke of my wearied and worried mother was God's gift, and was the chosen instrument of divine power through which God began a series of painful mortifications. I thank God for that astonishing conversation with my mom years ago, one I would hold dear, as she is dear to my heart.

In 1983, I was invited to preach in a town church, a small one with only thirty kind-hearted, dear people. Six months into seminary education, my head was bursting with an enormous amount of knowledge. To show off how much I had picked up in a short period, and impress upon them what a scholar they had in their pulpit, I started the illustration from reformation theology with an appalling statement: "Those of us who are well-versed in reformation theology. . . ." It is perfectly clear that no one person understands what reformation theology is all about, and neither did the man in the pulpit.

A week later, my history professor heard about this dreadful thing. He chastised me, "Dennis, I heard you are an expert in reformation theology."

"Oh! No," I answered shamefully.

"I thought not," he echoed.

Then he offered me a stern reproof, "In the future, Dennis, I would be much happier if you do not parade the learning you do not possess. Work hard at reformation theology, purify by it, and proclaim it."

In retrospect, I truly thank God for his straightforward stinging rebuke, which was God-sent. Later on, I went on and completed a PhD degree in theology, with a focus on Luther. Since then, I have published two major monographs on Luther, with the third one on its way.

In 2001, Dr. Jeff Greenman, my former dean and presently an associate dean of Wheaton College, took me into his office and challenged me to write. As is characteristic of a good dean, his words were demanding but thoughtful, "Dennis, you are already an established evangelist and teacher, but not an established scholar. After your first monograph in 1995, *The Suffering of God according to Martin Luther's Theologia Crucis*, have you ever thought of putting out another one? When you do, make sure that you send it out for scholarly peer reviews, for that would only make a better production as the outcome. Don't fall for a short-cut."

Keenly aware of my own insecurity, I replied, "Jeff, in five years, I shall have the second monograph out in print." Providentially the second monograph, *Apologetic for Filioque in Medieval Theology*, was published in 2005. I also completed the *Luther as A Spiritual Adviser* monograph in 2006, which was then published the following year.

In 2003, when Jeff recommended me to the Board of Governors as Research Professor of Theology, he asked me, "would you accept it?" With fear and trembling, I replied, "I would only assume it if I really publish." Since then, I have managed to publish two major peer-reviewed monographs, with a few more to complete. For years to come, I shall try to honor his commendation, and live up to his expectations, as I have so far.

Never undermine the efficacy of a wise rebuke, the instrument of divine causality. I am the byproduct of the *better way* propounded by the preacher of the Ecclesiastes, "It is better to hear the rebuke of the wise than the song of the fools."

The Heartbeat of a Mentor:
"The opposite of Love is not Rebuke, but Flattery"

Finally, let me speak with you as a mentor, if I may. Dear friends, this is the climactic word for you, the heartbeat of a mentor.

Beware of the smooth-talkers and sweet-talkers, with their oily politeness, who pamper you and butter you up with insincere comments and lies. Do not walk in the counsel of the ungodly. Away with mentors who are too affirming of your performances, but lack depth and discernment. Stay away from professors who gave your paper an A, without telling you how you have gotten there; but follow those who give your paper a B+, and show you how to excel and succeed. Away with those who cushion you with the melody of the fools, the faint praises by which many lives are ruined. Stay away from those who applaud mediocrity, celebrate superficiality, and entertain triviality. All these are an anti-climax, impediments to spiritual transformation and intellectual growth.

Cleave to these worthy servants we honor tonight; they are God's gifts to the church. Stay close to mentors who are honest, skilful, and audacious enough to correct you in order to lead you to a higher ground. Remember this: *the opposite of love is not rebuke, but flattery.*

Let us, as a community of faith, aspire to an evangelical identity constituted by an interface of scholarship and churchmanship. By God's grace, we shall strive to achieve the interaction of theology and piety, a distinctive mark of the Centre for Mentorship and Theological Reflection. Let us, as God's people, apply eagerly the gifts we have been endowed with for the defense of our faith and in the service of God's kingdom.

Appendix

CENTRE FOR MENTORSHIP AND THEOLOGICAL REFLECTION
"The Cross is Our Theology," Martin Luther

FOUNDER: *Dr. Dennis Ngien (PhD)*
Theology Professor, Preacher and Author

The CENTRE FOR MENTORSHIP AND THEOLOGICAL REFLECTION is an independent ministry, offering a learning experience in a context outside that of seminary or college, and specifically for those preparing for ministry, currently holding a formal position in ministry, or serving as lay leader.

The CENTRE sponsors table-talk mentorship on Bible-based Preaching (e.g., Galatians, 1 John, etc.), and supplies categories and materials for preaching and teaching.

The CENTRE provides individualized mentorship on specific needs or concerns (e. g., spiritual direction, preaching, apologetic issues, etc.), inculcating both spiritual and intellectual transformation.

The CENTRE assists needy churches in the areas of pulpit ministry, and leadership development, which may involve intern students in the process.

The CENTRE sponsors an Annual Theology and Worship Event, featuring renowned Scholar-Pastors, and on Special topics related to Church Life and Practice.

The CENTRE offers Research Scholarship Funds for sabbatical professors involved in research and publication, and confers Awards (e.g., Senior Scholar, Senior Churchman, etc.) to gifted leaders in recognition of their contributions in scholarship and service.